I0436277

Editor-in-Chief and Founder:
  Lyndon H. LaRouche, Jr.
Editorial Board: *Lyndon H. LaRouche, Jr. , Helga
  Zepp-LaRouche, Robert Ingraham, Tony
  Papert, Gerald Rose, Dennis Small, Jeffrey
  Steinberg, William Wertz*
Co-Editors: *Robert Ingraham, Tony Papert*
Managing Editor: *Nancy Spannaus*
Technology: *Marsha Freeman*
Books: *Katherine Notley*
Ebooks: *Richard Burden*
Graphics: *Alan Yue*
Photos: *Stuart Lewis*
Circulation Manager: *Stanley Ezrol*

INTELLIGENCE DIRECTORS
Counterintelligence: *Jeffrey Steinberg, Michele
  Steinberg*
Economics: *John Hoefle, Marcia Merry Baker,
  Paul Gallagher*
History: *Anton Chaitkin*
Ibero-America: *Dennis Small*
Russia and Eastern Europe: *Rachel Douglas*
United States: *Debra Freeman*

INTERNATIONAL BUREAUS
Bogotá: *Miriam Redondo*
Berlin: *Rainer Apel*
Copenhagen: *Tom Gillesberg*
Houston: *Harley Schlanger*
Lima: *Sara Madueño*
Melbourne: *Robert Barwick*
Mexico City: *Gerardo Castilleja Chávez*
New Delhi: *Ramtanu Maitra*
Paris: *Christine Bierre*
Stockholm: *Ulf Sandmark*
United Nations, N.Y.C.: *Leni Rubinstein*
Washington, D.C.: *William Jones*
Wiesbaden: *Göran Haglund*

ON THE WEB
e-mail: eirns@larouchepub.com
www.larouchepub.com
www.executiveintelligencereview.com
www.larouchepub.com/eiw
Webmaster: *John Sigerson*
Assistant Webmaster: *George Hollis*
Editor, Arabic-language edition: *Hussein Askary*

EIR (ISSN 0273-6314) *is published weekly
(50 issues), by EIR News Service, Inc.,
P.O. Box 17390, Washington, D.C. 20041-0390.
(703) 777-9451*

European Headquarters: E.I.R. GmbH, Postfach
Bahnstrasse 9a, D-65205, Wiesbaden, Germany
Tel: 49-611-73650
Homepage: http://www.eirna.com
e-mail: eirna@eirna.com
Director: Georg Neudecker

Montreal, Canada: 514-461-1557

Denmark: EIR - Danmark, Sankt Knuds Vej 11,
basement left, DK-1903 Frederiksberg, Denmark.
Tel.: +45 35 43 60 40, Fax: +45 35 43 87 57. e-mail:
eirdk@hotmail.com.

Mexico City: EIR, Sor Juana Inés de la Cruz 242-2
Col. Agricultura C.P. 11360
Delegación M. Hidalgo, México D.F.
Tel. (5525) 5318-2301
eirmexico@gmail.com

Canada Post Publication Sales Agreement
#40683579

Postmaster: Send all address changes to *EIR*, P.O.
Box 17390, Washington, D.C. 20041-0390.

Signed articles in *EIR* represent the views of the
authors, and not necessarily those of the Editorial
Board.

Obama Drives for War with China

EIR Contents

www.larouchepub.com Volume 43, Number 15, April 8, 2016

Cover
This Week

A U.S. Navy exercise in the South China Sea.

U.S. Navy photo, Intelligence Specialist 1st Class John J. Torres

I. Obama Drives for War with China

TO SAVE THE WORLD FROM THERMONUCLEAR WAR

Throw Obama out of the Presidency!

The following excerpts are taken from the March 31, 2016 Fireside Chat with Lyndon LaRouche, the April 2, 2016 Manhattan Project Dialogue, and an earlier, private discussion with Mr. LaRouche, also on April 2.

From the Fireside Chat

Lyndon LaRouche: I would say that right now we're going into a more deeply rooted crisis situation throughout not only the United States, but throughout much of the planet. We're on the edge of a threatened launching of war against China and implicitly also Putin, China in particular,— and the threats are becoming very serious. If these threats were to be carried out, the immediate effect would be a general thermonuclear war fought throughout the entire planet.

That is what the facts are, because if Putin were knocked out and if China was being hit directly, by Obama's directions, you would have the worst general warfare on the planet Earth that has ever occurred, that we have ever experienced. That's where we are.

The important thing is, I would say, is essentially to get the space program. What Kesha Rogers represents today, in terms of the Texas area, is a rebirth of the original space program. It's a modest one so far. It's not on as large a scale as it was then originally, but it is a fully qualified space program, and it's situated in Texas right now.... I think that's where we stand.

Question: This is R— from Brooklyn. Some of the media have been putting out such negative stuff on Putin, that it's fantastic. What can we do to overcome some of this stuff, and get over to people the sig-

nificance of not just Putin but the Chinese leadership and the other people that are involved, and the New Silk Road, and all this other related stuff that we want to get into our program?

LaRouche: The situation right now, is that Obama is actually in the process of pushing for a general war with China—*now!* This is what is happening now. There are other factors in this whole situation. It's a more complicated thing. Everybody is involved in this in some way or the other, for good or bad. But that's what the situation is.

As presented by the statements of President Obama, Obama has himself posed a proposal for thermonuclear war, a global thermonuclear war. Because any attack on China, from the United States, would be, from the opening, a general, global thermonuclear war. And the best way to save the world from that is to throw Obama out of the Presidency.

White House

LaRouche: Obama has already set into motion a general thermonuclear war throughout the planet. Get him out of there right away. Right away! Leave him in there and he's going to go for a thermonuclear war!

General War Against the Planet

Question: My name is E— from Eritrea. I think the BRICS program is a program of peace, of development for all nations, and it is headed by China. But some of the concern that I have is about Brazil, South Africa, and India: Those governments have problems of realizing the BRICS in a long-term venture, because I think, internally, they are not as stable as China and Russia. Do you think Brazil, India and South Africa will stay as honest partners of the venture, of the BRICS?

LaRouche: I would say the point is any brink of a major war, which involves Obama in particular, as the President of the United States, any launching of any such war, will be an immediate *global, general, all-out war;* a war worse than anything that mankind has experienced heretofore.

So there is no such thing as an option of taking some section of the world economy, some part of the economy of the world. It cannot be divided. If a war starts, Obama is ready to launch a *general war* against the planet! That's what's on the edge. So you have to *stop Obama totally.* If you don't, or if he is not stopped by some other influence, then you are into a general, global war, a thermonuclear war, which will be throughout the planet. Don't be fooled by the idea of partial solutions, or partial options; they don't exist. If such a war occurs, and Obama is involved in that war, the war will be immediate, and obvious and total.

Question: Lyn, as you probably know, today Obama is involved in a summit meeting on nuclear security in Washington. There are fifty heads of state there, except that President Putin did not show up at the meeting. What would you say about the fact that President Putin did not come to Washington, in the face of Obama's so-called Nuclear Summit Meeting today?

LaRouche: There is a certain condition involved in this process, how this war, this new world war, could come about. First of all, *it's highly likely that such a war will be launched.* It is not certain that the *full-scale war* will be launched. The complication is that in the case of Putin, Putin would know, immediately, that if he supported China, where China has been subjected to a war launched by Obama, if Putin were to put a signal out

U.S. Air Force/Staff Sgt. Benjamin Sutton

A U.S. Air Force B-52 Stratofortress based on Guam conducts a low-level flight in the vicinity of Osan Air Base, South Korea, on Jan. 10, in response to a North Korean nuclear test.

that he is jumping in, to support China, from his, Putin's, position, that would only assure, guarantee, a general thermonuclear war globally and almost immediately.

Therefore, if he holds back on launching an initiative of this type, then the problem lies entirely with the responsibility of Obama. Now, if Obama goes alone in launching an attack on China, at least in the first phase, then there will be restraint, because there will be confusion. So what we want to do is think about the strategic ways in which to manage a general thermonuclear war. And that's what we're faced with.

If we were to have a general thermonuclear war breaking out, as from China, as well as Russia, and Russia as well as China, if that were to be just unleashed suddenly, you would have a terrible problem to deal with. So if Obama tries to push for launching *his* war against China, there are complications which would occur, which would tend to weaken the ability of Obama to launch a full-scale war. This is the only—I know it's complicated — but that's exactly what it is.

And the key thing is, if you want to do something about it,— well, the best thing you can do is for the United States to stop the war. If the officials of government in the United States were to say "no support for

LaRouche PAC

LaRouche: We must think of the strategic ways to manage a general thermonuclear war. That's what we are faced with.

Obama," that would work! That would really work! So that's the other aspect of the problem.

Question: All of the world's people need to work together to solve the problems we humans face together. If we continue to allow ourselves to be torn apart, with our resources plundered to support these endless wars, we face certain destruction. We must stand together against this danger. If we continue to allow ourselves to be divided by the psychopaths, we will die divided and alone. Unite to save our future!

Mr. LaRouche, who are the psychopaths trying to divide us, and how do we act to make sure we are united to save the future?

Putin Is No Dummy

LaRouche: That's a complicated question to ask because there are elements in that which are not quite accurate. You cannot get people to work together and solve this problem. That you cannot do!—it will never succeed. There are things that you can do, which will succeed, but they have to be specific kinds of programs, assembled by a group of people who are supporting those programs.

You just cannot have a vote taken, "let's all go together out there and win the party." That does not work; it never did work, and it never will work.

You have to have to have an organization created, or developed, inside the United States and around it,

which does represent a very specific kind of reform. In other words, you cannot just go out there and say, "Let's agree to try to do everything for our common cause, despite whatever we have on our minds." That does not work. You have to have a mission-orientation.

Now, there's another aspect to this, which is even more profound. The question is, what makes mankind as a social process? What makes it worthwhile? It has to be something: How do you avoid a Roman Empire. How do we avoid something like that? Or a Satanic cult? How do you avoid that? You can't just say, "we'll all get together, we're good ol' fellows, we're going to solve our problems." That does not work.

You have to pick the right program. And you have to understand it. And when people get confused and allow themselves to be just swarmed by the common interest, that does not work. That results in the worst, it probably could lead to Satanic results, or other conditions.

You don't win unless you know what you're doing.

Question: This is T— from Lake Arrowhead, California. I just heard on the news that President Putin is not going to be attending Obama's Nuclear Security Summit, and there's going to be something like fifty world leaders there, including Xi Jinping. Do you have any thoughts as to why Vladimir Putin has decided to boycott this particular nuclear security conference?

LaRouche: He's not doing any such thing. He's not avoiding something. What he's doing is stepping aside, to allow a larger process to go into work.

Putin is a very sharp person; he's not a dummy! He's probably one of the sharpest men on the planet. So be very careful about how you should criticize how he works.

You know I never spoke to him personally, but I know him very well. He and I were actually in a parallel operation for a period of time; he was doing some things at one time, in that place, and I was, at the same time, doing something similar in a different place! And that's how we got to know each other without actually talking to each other directly.

This Putin is not any scamp of any kind! He's real! And anyone who knows him, or knows the history of the recent period, would know that. *Putin is not a joke!* He is not an option. He is a master operator. I don't know how smart he was before, but I know he's very smart right now!

The point is, Putin's position is, that he does not want to be an also-ran supporter of launching a war, to

Presidential Press and Information Office

LaRouche: Putin is drawing out opportunities to restrict the scope of the attempted launching of general thermonuclear war—by Obama. So Putin is a very smart gentleman. He knows that you don't try to increase the span of a war you don't want to spread. So, as long as Putin has a free hand, you have a way to break the immediacy of the general warfare.

defend China, because… then you would have a guaranteed global thermonuclear war, and it would be very quickly settled. Most of the people on the planet would be dead in a very short period of time.

So what Putin is doing, he's actually drawing out opportunities to restrict the scope of the attempt to launch a general thermonuclear war—*by Obama*. So Putin is a very smart gentleman and he knows the tricks. He knows that you don't try to increase the span of a war you don't want to spread. And that's exactly what's on his mind.

There are other factors in what is on his mind; there are different factors. But they all add up to the same general effect.

Question: This is E— in Los Angeles; I have two questions about Obama. My first question about Obama is, we know that he didn't go to Argentina to sing and dance. I think he went there to do everything he could to try to destroy the BRICS concept, now that they have a different government there, unfortunately. The second question about Obama, is, I am hearing from several sources, and they said they confirmed it, now I don't know if it's real or not,— that Obama is actually not even officially running the country any more. That they've installed Paul Ryan and a military man from the Joint Chiefs of Staff as Vice President. Now, this is

going around. Do you have any knowledge about this at all?

Obama a Mass Murderer

LaRouche: Well, this goes from the beginning. Obama did not become President in the usual way of becoming a President. He was stuck in there, and he was stuck in there by the Queen of England! He was a stooge for the Queen of England. And coming in as a stooge for the Queen of England, he would actually be on the pay and control of the British Queen at that time.

He's also a murderer, a mass murderer, because every Tuesday,—or at least what I've got from my last reports on it,— every Tuesday Obama kills American citizens and others, murders them. He is a stooge of the worst kind, and he does what the stooge bosses want.

He should have been dumped a long time ago. The British system, in creating the Obama Administration, which is what was done, was done as a way to try to destroy the United States,— in other words, to get a nominal President, who is not really a President by intention, but is an agent of the British Queen. Now, that's the case.

Now, of course there have been many cases in which agents of the British Queen have been controlling factors in the government of the United States. And he's one of them. So Obama is not real, that is, not real in the sense of anything. But the British system put the thing up: It was the British Empire that put Obama into power, along with [Valerie] Jarett and so forth, who are part of the stooges involved in that.

So what's happened is, the British Empire has managed to pull off a number of things, including the Saudi attack on the United States. In other words the Saudi government, under British direction, launched a war against the United States. Same thing.

So therefore, you've got to get the records clear, to realize what a complex kind of thing we're dealing with in this. But in the important phase, you have to understand what these factors are, so you don't get misled by your misinterpretation of these factors.

I could give you a lot more on this thing, but that's essentially the hard case.

Question: This is E—. I'm a freelance national security reporter and former staff reporter. I've been following your work closely since the Benghazi attacks [Sept. 11, 2012], and I'm very interested in what you have to say.

My question is, if Obama were to be impeached or were to leave office before this year's elections commence, what do you foresee happening? What would happen next, and what would be the implications for the United States and subsequently, the world?

LaRouche: If we were not to intervene, now, and Obama were to act as he intends to act right now—as a matter of fact Obama has already set into motion a general thermonuclear war throughout the planet. Now, the question whether he'll succeed in doing that or not, is another question, but the fact is, he's doing it, and he is putting military forces, a lot of them, into it. And that's the intention.

In the meantime, you find that the entirety of the trans-Atlantic community is a disaster. Everything that we had beforehand has just crashed; we're losing everything.

So we have two things: Get Obama out of there, right away. *Right away!* Leave him in there and he's going to go for a thermonuclear war! So you've got to get him out of there. Once you do that, take that step, then you have to take reconstruction kinds of measures, and those measures are possible, they're feasible. It's going to take the willingness of the people, themselves, to decide to accept those revisions of the thing.

From the Manhattan Dialogue

Question: This is J—, from Brooklyn. What I wanted to ask about, today, while we were actually singing our concert, and praising God, and bringing people from the community into the church, to celebrate peace and prosperity, and send out the word about the Silk Road and the things we're working on, it seems that there was an article that appeared in the London *Economist*—and I've also heard it was in the *Washington Post*—that actually threatened the life of the Chinese leader, Xi Jinping, and his family. People are asking why didn't Putin attend this so-called Nuclear Summit that Obama put together. I'd like you to address that situation, about Putin's strategic "non-attendance." And, the fact that, they're saying that there's a "defector" that wrote this article, or made sure this article got placed in these newspapers. And, this defector

from China threatened the life of the leader of China, and his family.

My take on it is that it's Obama, and since Obama is a stooge for the British Empire, it's the British Empire that put this out. There is no "defector." These are the kinds of things they do in order to get their nonsense out into the public, into the world. And, the strategic situation with Putin is very important, as to why he did not attend this summit. And if you comment on that?

Obama an Enemy of the United States

LaRouche: I just stated this past Thursday, what my policy was, that we did not want to get Putin to come in on that action. That is, we "duck it," in a sense—because we know what it is. It's a fraud. We don't want him to respond.

Since Putin has a leading position in Europe in general, and the record he has of what he's done, there's no need for us to suggest his role in this thing. He will act in good time. He's not a man who panics. He does what he has to do, when he has to do it. And, people can't lock him into falling into some trap.

So, what happens is, the attack on the leadership of China is a very serious threat. It's a threat *by Obama.* Now, any American citizen who hears this, should realize this guy is an enemy. If he's trying to make an enemy of China, then he should be thrown out of office! Period.

Because nations have to cooperate. Whether they like each other or not, is not the question. Do they maintain the kind of relationship which is necessary for nations to work together?

Obama is an evil man. He is a Satanic figure, among a number of Satanic figures which we know in the world. He should have been thrown out of the Presidency. There's no good reason he hasn't been thrown out of the Presidency. And the Bushes are also in there.

But Obama is a *Satanic creature,* and should be treated as such. It's the only way to do it. The people of the United States should reject Obama, throw him out, because he's a Satanic figure, and that is not an exaggeration.

He has done more to destroy the welfare of the people of the United States than any other single case on record. Just think of the number of Americans that have been destroyed by Obama! Just think of the number of people who are dying, by the cause of Obama's behavior. He's the enemy of the United States! And anyone who doesn't recognize that, is not a loyal citizen of the United States.

U.S. Navy/Mass Communication Specialist 2nd Class Ryan J. Batchelder

Obama is provoking China in the South China Sea, looking for a rumble, claiming that the United States must police these waters to preserve freedom of trade and travel. Here, the guided-missile cruiser USS Mobile Bay (foreground) in the South China Sea on March 4, 2016, replenishing fuel and stores of fast combat support ship USNS Rainier.

Question: Hello, Lyn, A— here, in New York. What J— began today's meeting with, I was very struck by, when you raised it on the phone, on Thursday, because that type of analysis, or understanding, of what Putin was actually doing, through his absence, of avoiding war—what you say would otherwise trigger, in the insane mind of Obama, an immediate response to go after both China and Russia.

Now, China is being attacked on three fronts, and they're all being highlighted in the work that we're doing: politically, economically, and now, militarily. You mentioned one thing on the phone that did throw me, and I rewrote it, you said, "We have to think in terms of strategic ways to manage thermonuclear war." And I said, so, what do you mean? I don't understand that.

Dump Obama!

LaRouche: There's a lot in warfare built up in the nations of the planet. And the question is, can you get them to control themselves and not to turn these potential wars, or warfare-like postures, into an actual war. That's the point. How do you get a peace out of a rage-fit among nations? And that's extremely important. Therefore, you have to get the lesson across, respecting

policy: *Nations must understand the interest of humanity first.* If they can't respond to the purposes of humanity, as such, you've got Hell!

And, therefore, you can go all the way up to the firing lines, *but if you don't go further, you will save civilization.* And therefore, we do have to avoid conflict, we do have to avoid killing, but we do have to find a resolution no matter how hostile the issue is.

The British Empire, for example,— now I know all about the British empire, and the British empire is Satanic. Now just the fact that the Queen of England is a Satanic figure is not a reason to go killing her. It's a reason to control her, to check her, and to prevent her from causing the kinds of things that will kill people and destroy their rights. Unless she commits a worse crime; in that case, she could be put in prison. No reason not to. Most of the Royal Family of Britain should be imprisoned; they should not be on the streets. They should be imprisoned, maybe up in that nest they have up there in the middle of nowhere.

But no, killing people is not the way to solve the problems, or trying to kill people. The point is to try to create a process of constraint, which constrains people out of will, or out of other kinds of compulsion, to prevent them from doing the commission of crimes.

Question: Good afternoon, Lyn. Given that Obama wants thermonuclear war and will go through any means, now the focus will be North Korea and Ukraine: Neither country can stand on its own to launch a war without U.S. intervention. North Korea is on the verge of another famine and has alerted their populace to prepare to eat grass and roots. Ukraine's economy has completely fallen apart. The IMF has broken its own rules of never lending money to a country that can't pay its debts.

My question is, how far is the United States going to go to intervene in both North Korea and Ukraine, to start thermonuclear war? Because obviously it's not going to be those two countries to do it, it's going to be the United States?

LaRouche: The point is very simple: Dump Obama! There's no reason for him to be there! He's only a delusion, and a disease. Obama is something who should never have existed as a President. The crimes he's committed, on Tuesdays, the number of innocent people he has killed, on his order! There's no reason for his being anywhere in the political system of the United States.

But if it were not for the corrupt elements, the really corrupt elements of the United States, we would not have that kind of problem. There's something wrong with the government of the United States, if it allows Obama to continue to exist.

Question: Good afternoon, R— here, from Brooklyn. With China's participation in the New Silk Road, aiming to end poverty in China by the year 2020, and worldwide by 2025, we have real hope for the world. Obama's anti-China rhetoric at the nuclear meeting this week is a clue as to where he is at. Are we making progress in getting rid of Obama?

LaRouche: Well, we should get rid of Obama, why didn't we do it? We've come to almost the end of his second term in the Presidency, and he's done more damage to the Presidency of the United States than any one individual in recent times. Why do you let this bum in there? Why did we let a man who on his Tuesday events, would actually celebrate the assassination of innocent members of our nation, kill them? On Tuesdays?

Question [follow-up]: I think a lot of Americans fell for the con job that he perpetrated.

LaRouche: It was worse. It was terror. It was not a con job, it was a *terror* job. It was a systemic terror! And other people in government watched this terror, and condoned it.

Obama could not have existed as he has, if the government of the United States, in the large part, did not defend and condone Obama for the crimes he committed! I mean, those of us who have been well-informed, know exactly what Obama did. We know who he was, we know what he did! We know it accurately, because we had access to the kind of information needed to know this.

So the problem is, the people of the United States have been terrified by the Obama Administration. The Bush family was an attempt at that kind of terror, but that didn't work too well. Obama did: Obama is the Satan of the United States: Get rid of him!

U.S. Navy

A U.S. guided-missile destroyer in the Pacific uses its Terminal High Altitude Area Defense (THAAD) and Ballistic Missile Defense (BMD) systems to defeat two nearly simultaneous practice targets.

From the April 2nd Private Discussion

LaRouche: I think that what I did Thursday evening [Fireside Chat] is probably one of the most important things to be re-examined and considered. Not because I did it, but because what I did actually went directly to the immediate issue throughout our entire nation. I mean, the entirety of it. These issues that I raised are probably the most crucial things that we can discuss, because everything is implicitly there in it. What I did Thursday night is the statement of what the issue is today. Just take that thing itself and examine it, reflect upon it, and you will find out that that one thing which I did is the most important thing I've done for a long time. Some people have recognized that, and some people will recognize it. That's who we are, and that's what the challenge is. Because it's not our challenge, as such. It's a general challenge—an existing challenge—which is not limited to what I said. What I said was simply something which fed into presenting the reality of the situation as it stood, and it will stay today.

We're on the edge of the most dangerous period in history, right now. And what I laid out Thursday night is the most important thing laid out in a long time, because I got enough in there to present the case. All the other things that people say, "Well, yes, but.... Yes, but.... Yes, but....," you say, "Horns don't work that well."

I think it would be an open question of discussion, at least at this moment, to review that consideration. Because all these kinds of ifs, and buts, and so forth—forget it! It's a done job. How the thing will work out is not known, but the intention is a done job. And Obama essentially has proposed a global thermonuclear war to occur now. That could be stopped, but there has to be a consciousness of the fact that this *is* something that has to be stopped. I think that's the discussion point which is of importance. You know what my thoughts are on this subject, and I've stated them repeatedly, so I don't

Unsurvivable

A dark, gruesome, but wholly true depiction of the threat of thermonuclear war, its consequences, and Obama's deployment of a major portion of the U.S. thermonuclear capabilities in multiple theaters threatening both Russia and China.

http://larouchepac.com/unsurvivable

need to keep repeating it indefinitely. All I have to do is re-warm your review of this reality.

We're on the edge of a thermonuclear war, globally. Can we stop it? It could be stopped. But you've got to take into account the factors which could stop it. That's what is the only important subject right now. That's it! We're on the edge of a general, global warfare. That is, the factor in there of Obama, and what Obama represents, together with the British empire, the British System, is exactly what the issue is. We're on the edge of Hell.

The Edge of Thermonuclear War

LaRouche: It's a simple question. Putin is allied with China—obviously. However, what if Putin and China go together to take an action, a common action? Well, that would probably be a mistake to do that, because if you create a situation where you have one enemy—that is, the British system—and that one enemy is focused on that subject, then it's very difficult to avoid an early war. What you want to do, is you want to cause the war that they're out to launch—which is a global war, a general warfare—and you've got something in the reverse, which is there, ready, to do something. Therefore, you hold that back up to an appropriate point. I think that is the best term, the appropriate point. In that way, you do not get the complete focus of a global warfare. If you take it and break it down into a different way, where the issue is China, and then what's Putin going to do?

That's the question. So, as long as Putin has a free hand in his own part, then you have a way to break the immediacy of the general warfare. That's why I put that emphasis in there. You cannot play toy soldiers with this kind of stuff.

We're on the edge of everything. That's a fact. So, don't think that there's one thing that might tip things off. Everything could tip things off. It's a question of how you try to avoid going into the wrong battlefield, or at least at the wrong time. The right battlefield at the wrong time is not good.

LaRouche: Well, we're at the edge of a general thermonuclear war. That's exactly what the situation is. It's not established, but all the factors are there.... This is a doom of all war. There's no limit on the war. There's no parameters. This is a reckless war, absolutely reckless. The United States does not have the kind of organization which is suited to conducting a major war. So what is it? The only thing is desperation warfare.

Every Day Counts In Today's Showdown To Save Civilization

That's why you need EIR's **Daily Alert Service**, a strategic overview compiled with the input of Lyndon LaRouche, and delivered to your email 5 days a week.

For example: On Jan. 7, EIR's Daily Alert featured the British hand behind the pattern of global provocations toward war. Of special note is British Intelligence's role in instigating the Saudi Kingdom's attempt to set off a Sunni-Shia war. This religious war has been the intent of British strategy since the Blair-Bush attack on Iraq in 2003.

We also uniquely update you regularly on the progress toward the release of the suppressed 28 pages of the Congressional Inquiry on 9/11, which would expose the Saudi role.

Every edition highlights the reality of the impending financial crash/bail-in policies that would realize the British goal of mass depopulation.

This is intelligence you need to act on, if we are going to survive as a nation and a species. Can you really afford to be without it?

THURSDAY, JANUARY 7, 2016

Volume 2, Number 97

EIR Daily Alert Service

P.O. Box 17390, WASHINGTON, DC 20041-0390

- British Crown Pushing War and Genocide in 2016
- Financial Mudslide Goes On; Monetarist Tyranny Gloats over Bail-Ins
- Moody's Downgrades Portugal's Novo Banco
- Puerto Rico's Default: It's Every Vulture for Himself
- Wide Glass-Steagall Debate Set Off Again by Sanders Speech
- MI6 Mouthpiece Evans-Pritchard Touts Persian Gulf Chaos
- North Korea Tests a Miniaturized Hydrogen Bomb
- Uighur Terrorists Found in Indonesia
- Foreign Investors Are Flocking In to China

EDITORIAL

British Crown Pushing War and Genocide in 2016

Development or War in Asia?

by Michael Billington

April 2—Since Obama's 2012 declaration of a "Pivot to Asia," this war-hungry President has "pivoted" nothing. Rather, he has maintained and even expanded his (and Bush's) policy of perpetual war in the Mideast, while also expanding the deployment of strategic forces in Europe right up to the Russian border. Nonetheless, Obama has also greatly expanded the U.S. military posture in Asia, and, in the past few months, is driving for a massive military encirclement of China along its entire coast, preparing for a thermonuclear assault on China.

In 2013, soon after Obama launched the "Pivot," Chinese President Xi Jinping announced his ambitious and optimistic plan for a New Silk Road Economic Belt—rail and development corridors from China through Central Asia and the Mideast to Europe (**Figure 1**)—and the Twenty-first Century Maritime Silk Road through the South China Sea, the Indian Ocean, the Persian Gulf and the Red Sea, connecting with the over-

land Silk Road in the Mediterranean countries. Together they are known as "One Belt, One Road."

This plan reflected the proposal issued by Lyndon and Helga LaRouche in the early 1990s following the collapse of the Soviet Union, to recreate the ancient Silk Road as the basis for uniting East and West in a joint development process, as the necessary precondition for ending once and for all the threat of thermonuclear war between the superpowers, and launching a new renaissance uniting all cultures based on the common aims of Mankind.

Russia was at that time being looted by western scavengers, and was in no position to adopt the proposal. The United States and its NATO allies rejected it altogether, choosing instead to follow the British Imperial policy of keeping the world divided against itself, as a means of control through their centralized global financial system.

FIGURE 1

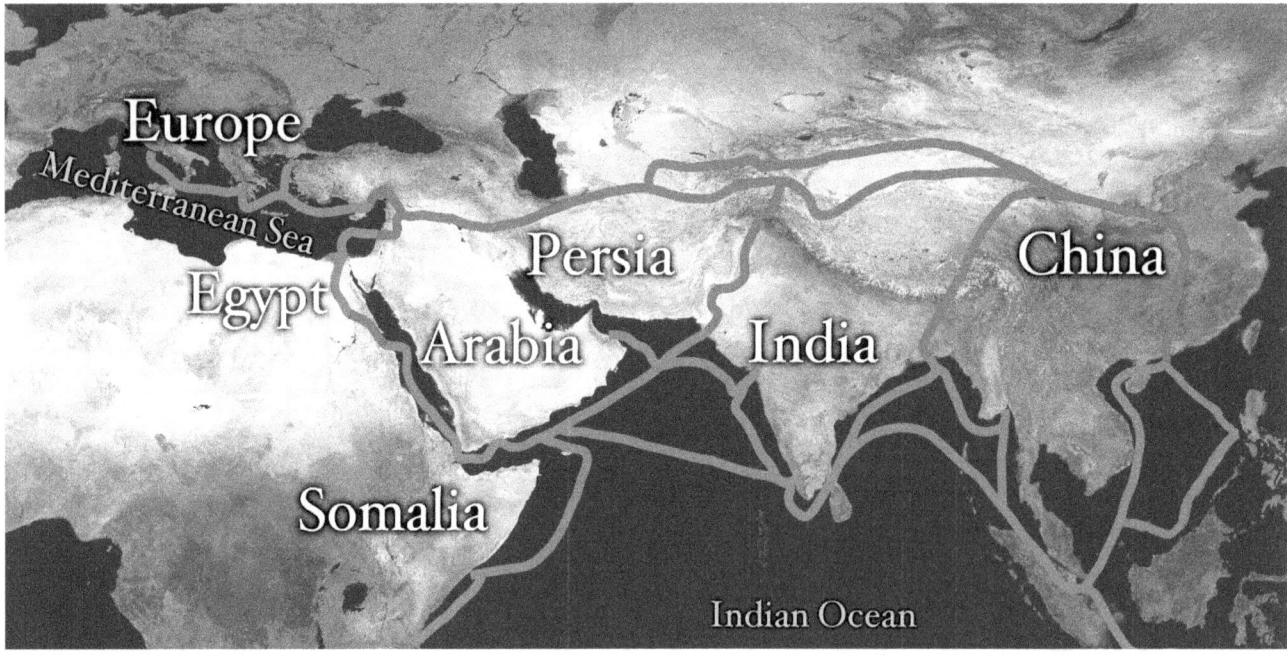

FIGURE 2

FIGURE 3

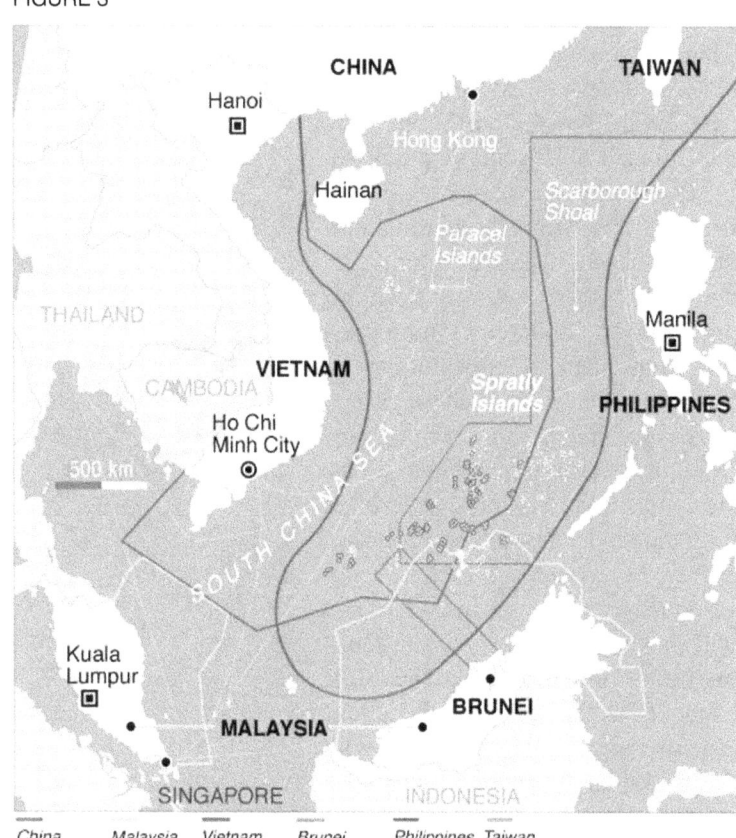

China, on the other hand, enthusiastically adopted the proposal, calling it the Eurasian Land-Bridge, and co-sponsored with Helga Zepp-LaRouche's Schiller Institutes a Eurasian Land-Bridge Conference in Beijing in 1996. Mrs. LaRouche was a leading organizer and a speaker for that conference.

Now, China's President Xi Jinping has restored LaRouche's preferred name—the New Silk Road—and linked this new development paradigm with major new credit institutions: the Asian Infrastructure Investment Bank (AIIB), the BRICS New Development Bank, and several funds linked to the nations of the Shanghai Cooperation Organization and to the Association of Southeast Asian Nations (ASEAN), among others, totaling hundreds of billions of dollars for global development.

To the bankrupt financial lords of Wall Street and the City of London, this development policy is seen as a threat, which must be crushed through economic and military confrontation.

Imperial Targets

There are three primary points of attack in Obama's confrontation with China (**Figure 2**):

- The South China Sea
- The Southeast Asian nations
- The Korean Peninsula.

Lyndon LaRouche has long argued that the South China Sea must be regarded as an "Asian Lake," which of course requires that the nations adjoining the "Lake" view their common interests as more important than their parochial concerns. How does this fit with China's recent construction of artificial islands in the Spratly/ Nansha island group, which has been used by Obama and his controllers to accuse China of "aggression" and "militarization" of the South China Sea?

One of China's leading economists, Ding Yifan, addressing a Schiller Institute conference on the New Silk Road in San Francisco in November 2013, was asked about the danger of war. He responded (**Figure 3**):

"I can say a few words about that. The New Silk Road is also critical for Chinese strategic defense, because historically, the threat to China came over land, from the north, but since the Opium War [Britain's Opium War of 1840], the threat always comes from the sea, from the ocean, from the southeastern part of China. So, with the Obama Administration's pivot to Asia, China feels more pressure from Japan, from the military alliance between the United States and Japan, so the pressure comes also from the southeast part, while the New Silk Road is a big background for China to have some provisions of energy, of resources, for Chinese development, and by railroad China will have access to the European market. So this time, when the threat comes from the sea, from the southeastern part, China can resist with this background support."

This identifies China's strategic interest in securing peace in the South China Sea. It must be noted, of course, that while China claims sovereignty over the Spratly/Nansha islands, the Paracel/Xisha islands and others within their so-called "nine dash line" in the South China Sea, they have never challenged the other nations which have occupied and armed islands under their control, although they lie within the nine dash line China considers its sovereign territory. This includes the Philippines and Vietnam. Nor have they challenged other countries which have constructed or expanded islands by artificial means, also including the Philippines and Vietnam (**Figure 4**).

As to China "militarizing" the South China Sea, as is repeated *ad nauseam* by Obama and his fellow war hawks in the Congress, the Pentagon and the press,— China has for decades had minimal defenses on the island of Yongxing (called Woody Island in the West), the site of Sansha City, which is the administrative center of the Chinese islands in the South China Sea. The recent "discovery" of defenses on this island is a fraud.

FIGURE 4

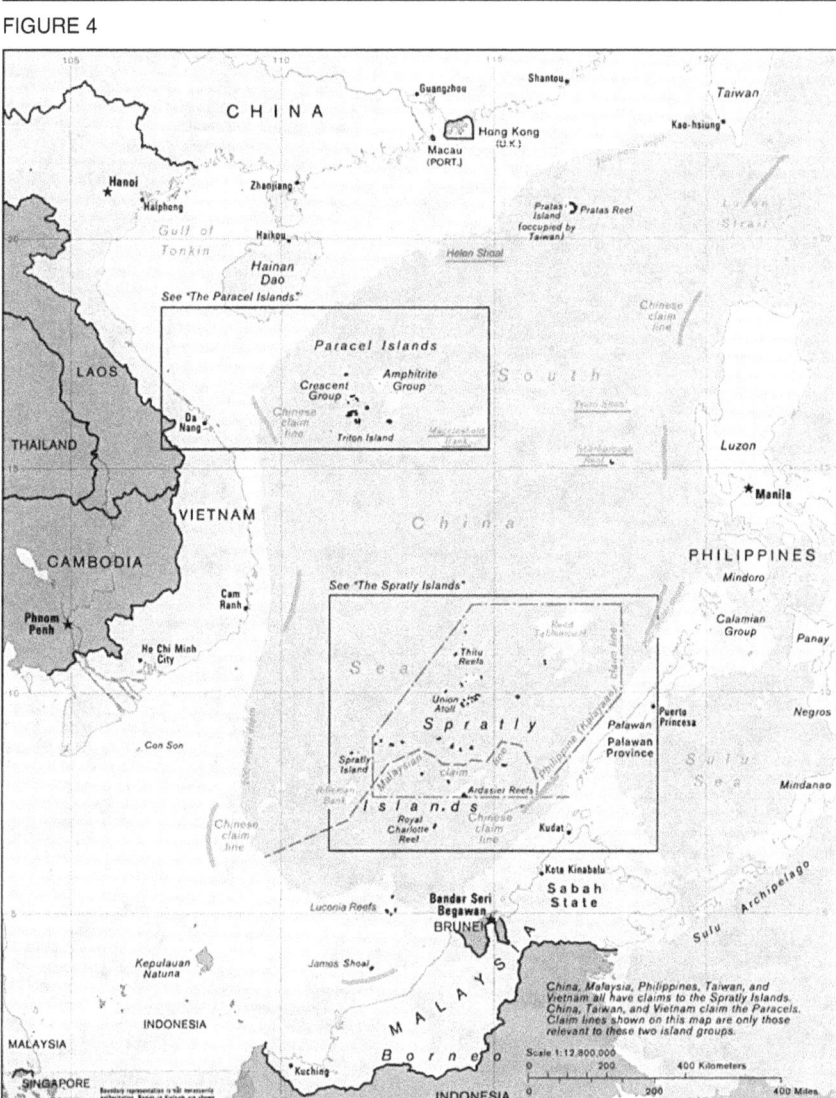

But Xi Jinping's pledge not to militarize the newly constructed islands in the Spratlys has been upheld, despite the hysterical screams in the West that China *might* deploy military forces to these tiny islands.

Contrast that to Obama's massive militarization of the South China Sea. Not only is Obama regularly and intentionally deploying warships and war planes into areas claimed by China in the region—for no other purpose than to militarily provoke China—but Obama has also in the last year successfully pressured the weak Philippine President Benigno "Noynoy" Aquino to disregard the Philippine Constitution, which forbids foreign troops or bases on its soil without Senate approval, by turning over five sites to the U.S. military to construct major military bases, pre-position war materials, and deploy the most modern and deadly air, sea, and land forces across their country—including a base on Palawan Island, which juts out into the South China Sea! It is clear to those who are not blind that this is preparation for war on China.

At this point, it is important to reflect on how Noynoy came to power. In 1986, the nation's last nationalist leader, Ferdinand Marcos, was overthrown in a coup run by a key founder of the U.S. neoconservative movement, George Shultz, then Secretary of State, and his deputy Paul Wolfowitz (later famous as the architect of the criminal war on Iraq in 2003). Lyndon LaRouche at the time had provided backing and advice to Marcos and his circle on the development of the nation. Marcos had built the first nuclear plant in Southeast Asia, had a master plan for industrialization, and made the Philippines self sufficient in rice—in fact, the economic development under Marcos made the Philippines the most admired nation in Southeast Asia at the time, even by South Korea. When LaRouche defended Marcos against the foreign-instigated coup (which was among the first of the "color revolutions" by the United States), he warned that the country would collapse into economic decay and chaos were the Marcos policies to be reversed.

Following the coup against Marcos, Cory Aquino, the mother of the current President, was placed in power. She immediately followed the dictates of the neocons in Washington, shutting down the completed nuclear power plant, ending the rice self sufficiency program, and scrapping the industrialization program. Rather than being the envy of all of Asia, the Philippines is now the basket case of ASEAN, sharing in none of the Silk Road development taking place across ASEAN with Chinese support. And, it has turned itself into cannon fodder for Obama's war on China.

ASEAN

The story is totally different for the other members of the ten-nation ASEAN. Obama attempted to corral the ASEAN leaders into an anti-China declaration at his Summit with ASEAN leaders at Sunnylands, California in February, but failed miserably. While none of the other ASEAN nations want to break ties with the United States, for obvious reasons, they are at the same time enthusiastically expanding their relations with China, and reject all efforts to prevent it.

The reasons are clear—while the United States is an important trade partner for ASEAN, and invests in extracting raw materials, it long ago gave up on building any infrastructure in Asia (or anywhere else in the world), while making extreme demands (and often imposing onerous sanctions) to impose Washington's view of democracy, human rights, and the environment. This is equally true of the IMF and the World Bank, which support "poverty alleviation" and environmental policies, but build virtually no infrastructure, thus keeping countries backward, without real development.

China is not interested in imperial demands, but in addressing the most fundamental human right, that of economic development, and in conditions which respect the dignity of man through participation in the progress of one's nation.

Look at the record in Southeast Asia, even before the Silk Road process and the AIIB are fully operative:

Indonesia: China Railway International and a consortium of Indonesian state companies won a contract in October 2015 to build Indonesia's first high-speed rail line, from Jakarta to Bandung, and plan to compete for other projects in the region. Three quarters of the funding will come from the China Development Bank. China won the contract against a viable Japanese bid primarily because China did not demand a guarantee for the project from the Indonesian government, which suffered total destruction in the 1998 "Asia Crisis" due to foreign contracts which had forced all the risk onto the government. This new contract for the Jakarta-Bandung Railroad is seen as a model for others among the Silk Road nations.

China has also built numerous power plants across Indonesia and has invested in port development. They completed construction of the longest bridge in the country in 2009, connecting Surabaya on the island of Java to Madura Island off the north coast. The *Jakarta Post* reported on Feb. 3 that since the sixtieth anniversary celebration in April 2015 of the famous Bandung *Asian African Conference*, "China has made a clean sweep of big infrastructure projects in Indonesia."

President Joko Widodo has a vision of Indonesia becoming a "maritime fulcrum" for the Pacific-Indian Ocean, which he considers to be congruent with Xi Jinping's Maritime Silk Road. In fact, President Xi first announced the Maritime Silk Road while addressing the Indonesian Parliament in October 2013.

China to Singapore Railway: China is in the process of building a rail link from Kunming in Yunnan Province to Singapore (**Figure 5**), passing through Laos, Thailand, and Malaysia, a 3,000 km connection.

FIGURE 5

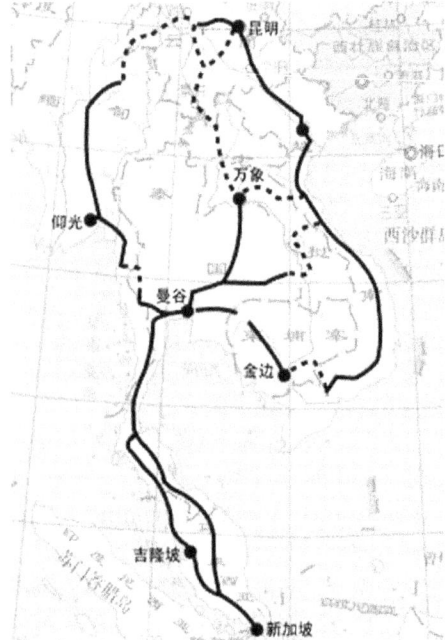

FIGURE 6

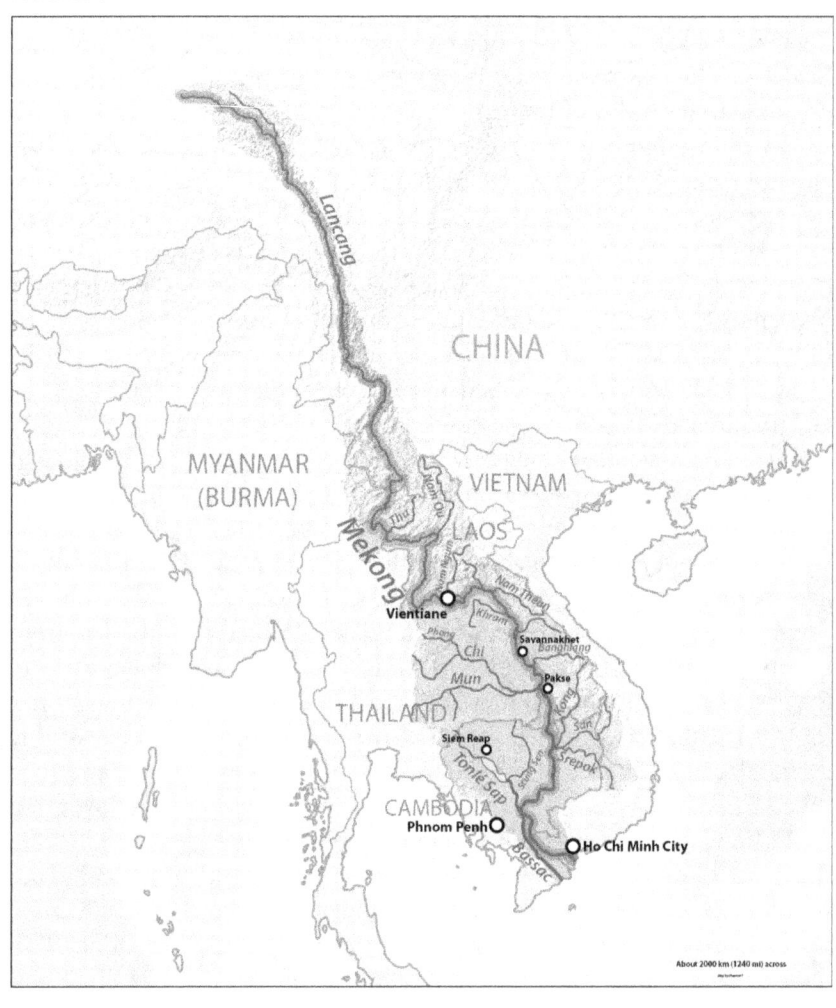

China and Laos broke ground on the 427 km high speed line connecting China to the Laotian capital of Vientiane near the Thai border in December. In Thailand, China has contracted to build a rail line from the Laos border to Bangkok, with a branch to the industrial center at Map Ta Phut, an ocean port southeast of Bangkok.

Bangkok-Kuala Lumpur: While a modern rail connection between Bangkok, Thailand, and Kuala Lumpur, Malaysia, is not yet in the works, a contract for the link from Kuala Lumpur to Singapore should soon be signed. China Railway Construction Corp in December bought into a major real estate venture called Bandar Malaysia in Kuala Lumpur, and in March announced that they were setting up a regional hub there, aiming at winning the rail contract and making Bandar Malaysia the terminal for the Kuala Lumpur-Singapore high-speed rail link.

Thailand and the Mekong: Besides the rail connections, the Thai Prime Minister, former General Prayut Chan-ocha, who directed a military coup in Thailand in 2013 to end the massive upheaval and near-civil war conditions in the country, has made relations with China a priority (**Figure 6**). In March, Prayut co-chaired with Chinese Premier Li Keqiang

the first summit of the Lancang-Mekong Cooperation, an organization of the six nations along the Mekong (China, Myanmar, Laos, Thailand, Cambodia, and Vietnam) held in Sanya, in China's Hainan Province (the Mekong is called the Lancang in China). The new insititution is essentially intended to coordinate the implementation of the Silk Road and the AIIB in the Mekong region.

As *EIR* reported in its landmark study, *The New Silk Road Becomes the World Land-Bridge*, see www. worldlandbridge.com, when the French were defeated in their colonial war in Vietnam in 1955, the United States sent engineers from FDR's great TVA project and from the Army Corps of Engineers to study the potential for reproducing the TVA process on the Mekong. They proposed an Indicative Basin Plan for 1970-2000, a project to produce 17,000 MW of hydropower with a ten-fold increase in irrigation during the dry season, doubling or tripling the productivity of that land.

With the assassination of John Kennedy and the launching of the Indochina War, the United States turned to a British colonial policy, waging war rather than fostering development. Even after losing that war in 1975, the United States never returned to its roots as a force for development, but sank deeper and deeper into permanent warfare and financial speculation.

As a result, it was admitted by the Mekong River Commission in its 2013 report, that "management and development of the River remains limited today, in part due to unregulated river flows. The vast floodplains in Cambodia remain largely undeveloped and only a small proportion of the irrigation, hydropower, and navigation potential has been realized in the basin. The River remains mostly in its natural state." The promise for development, once identified with the United States, has been abandoned in the West, but is now being taken up by China, with the enthusiastic support of the nations of Southeast Asia.

Lyndon LaRouche has been directly involved in promoting development in Thailand since the early 1980s, when *EIR* co-sponsored forums in Bangkok presenting detailed engineering studies for the construction of the Kra Canal—connecting the South China Sea and the Indian Ocean by cutting a canal across the Ishthmus of Kra in southern Thailand, above the Malacca Strait. The Canal would cut 900 miles from the trip through the Malacca Strait, far less than the distance saved by the Suez and Panama canals, but would nonetheless carry as much traffic as those canals because of the overcrowding of the Malacca Strait. LaRouche emphasized a more important aspect, that the Kra Canal "should be seen as a keystone, around which might be constructed a healthy and balanced development of needed infrastructure in a more general way."

The Canal is also the unique means to end the insurgency in the south of Thailand, providing jobs, new cities and ports, and development zones—another example of peace through development.

Although the plan was close to implementation in the 1980s, with significant Japanese interest, the potential disappeared with the economic crises of the late Twentieth Century. Now, with China also showing great interest, the plan is back on the table, and can serve as a major hub of the new Asia-Pacific Basin development.

China is also massively invested in Cambodia and Myanmar, building dams, power plants, roads, oil pipelines, and more. Cultural and educational exchanges are being implemented across the region.

Of course, China is not the only country investing in ASEAN. Japan and South Korea are also building infrastructure, including transportation, water projects, and power plants. But the West no longer builds infrastructure, which is left to the private sector, which is not interested in investments that take several decades to develop. Infrastructure does not return short-term profits to a private investor, but rather generates an increase in the productivity of the nation and region as a whole. Americans once understood this, as government investment fueled every period of American progress, and the lack of such government backing drove every period of collapse. The key to peace and development lies in lifting the vision of men and nations to the future.

Korea

We are now seeing the threat of a crisis in the Korean Peninsula serving as an excuse for a global war, launched by the United States against China. Obama was using the Syria crisis in a similar manner, as a cockpit for war against Russia—until Putin's military intervention exposed Obama's support for terrorists as allies in his drive for regime change against Assad.

And yet, just months ago, South Korea was working closely with China and Russia, and indirectly with North Korea, on development projects which were leading to a "peace through development" solution to this festering remnant of the Cold War. The recent nucear and missile tests in North Korea—which no one of sound mind could have doubted would eventually take place—were used by Obama to successfully coerce South Korean President Park Geun-hye to totally scrap these policies. The long-standing Kaesong Industrial Region, where South Korea factories were functioning in the North with North Korea labor, a win-win policy, was unilaterally shut down by Seoul.

Obama is also preparing to move THAAD (Terminal High Altitude Area Defense) missiles into South Korea, which South Korea had strongly opposed before President Park's capitulation. Park had earlier recognized that high altitude missiles are of essentially no use against North Korea, which does not need ICBMs to attack the South, but are in fact targetting China, just as the missiles deployed on Russia's border in Europe were falsly claimed by Obama to be needed to defend against Iran, when they were clearly aimed at Russia.

Then, by imposing additional South Korean sanctions, above and beyond the UN sanctions against North Korea of March 2, President Park has shut down the crucial cooperation between China, Russia, and both Koreas which was centered at Rason, a port city in northeast North Korea. China had built a road from its Jilin Province to Rason, while Russia had rebuilt the rail connection from Vladivostok through Kasan to Rason, and both Russia and China built port facilities there.

Most important, three major South Korean firms—Hyundai Marine, Korail (the state rail company), and Posco (one of the world's largest steel companies)—had formed a consortium with Russia and North Korea, with the approval of Seoul. The consortium had been shipping Russian coal by rail to Rason, where it was loaded on Hyundai Marine ships for transport to South Korea, then shipped by Korail to Posco plants. Such win-win cooperation between the nations of East Asia was potentially leading to the reconstruction of the rail lines through North Korea, which would complete the Eurasian Land-Bridge from Pusan, South Korea to Rotterdam, Holland, as envisaged by Lyndon LaRouche

and others as the crucial completion of the New Silk Road for Eurasian cooperation and peace.

This optimistic process is presented in detail in the *EIR* Special Report, *The New Silk Road Becomes the World Land-Bridge*, which is due to be published in a Korean translation within the coming weeks. Never has this policy been more needed than now.

While the West blames all this on North Korea for refusing to unilaterally give up its nuclear weapons program, it is obvious that North Korea has observed how the United States treated Iraq and Libya after they gave up their nuclear weapons programs. Obama's insane "strategic patience" approach to North Korea was simply a policy of preventing any constructive dialogue, allowing North Korea to continue its nuclear weapons program to justify the continuing, and now escalating, military build-up around China.

The future of mankind now rests squarely on the question facing the citizens of the world: Do we allow the world to sleepwalk into World War Three under Obama, or do we bring sanity back to the United States and Europe, and join with China and the BRICS in creating a future based on the advancement of the common aims of Mankind?

Thermonuclear War or "Win-Win" Cooperation with the New Silk Road

by Helga Zepp-LaRouche, chair of the German political party
Civil Rights Movement Solidarity

April 1—Disguised under doublespeak—window-dressing on the one hand and blatant threats on the other—the Obama Administration, egged on by British Prime Minister David Cameron, is currently pursuing a broad array of strategic confrontations with Russia and China, which aim at cementing the United States' claims to a unipolar world. The Pentagon's decision to station a full U.S. armored brigade, beginning in early 2017, along the border the Baltic states share with Russia, is a case in point. So also is the prospect of the U.S. stationing the mobile THAAD missile defense system in South Korea—a decision which China decisively rejects because its range strongly affects Chinese security interests. There are also the ongoing provocations in the South China Sea, be it the refusal to recognize China's right to establish an Air Defense Identification Zone or the setting up of naval and airborne reconnaissance patrols under the pretext of the need to defend the "freedom of navigation," which China is not challenging at all.

Timed with the Fourth Nuclear Security Summit in Washington, held March 31-April 1, President Obama wrote in an op-ed in the *Washington Post* that he had ruled out the development of new nuclear warheads and had also narrowed the contingencies for the use or the threat of use of nuclear weapons. The problem with this assertion is that, to put it diplomatically, it is false: The Obama Administration has not only allocated about $350 billion for the modernization of nuclear weapons, but the relevant programs would make these weapons more usable, just as Hans Kristensen of the Federation of American Scientists, among others, has repeatedly pointed

out. In his March 25 blog posting, Kristensen reported on a hearing in the Senate Appropriations Committee, during which Senator Dianne Feinstein decisively contradicted officials of the Obama Administration, who were defending the modernization. She said: "The so-called improvements to this weapon [meaning the B61-12 bombs stationed in Germany and the Long Range Standoff Cruise Missiles—ed.] seem to be designed candidly to make it more usable, to help us fight and win a limited nuclear war. I find that a shocking concept. I think this is really unthinkable, especially when we hold conventional weapons superiority, which can meet adversaries' efforts to escalate a conflict … because this just ratchets up warfare, and ratchets up deaths."

Sen. Dianne Feinstein (D-Ca.), the ranking member of the Senate Appropriations Committee, on March 16: "The so-called improvements to this weapon [the B61-12 bombs and the Long Range Standoff Cruise Missiles] seem to be designed candidly to make it more usable, to help us fight and win a limited nuclear war. I find that a shocking concept."

U.S. Department of State

U.S. Secretary of State John Kerry, Russian Foreign Minister Sergey Lavrov, and German Foreign Minister Frank-Walter Steinmeier stressed Russia's role in enabling a political solution in Syria, in a joint press conference. Here they take their seats at the March 24 meeting in Moscow. From left, Steinmeier and Lavrov. Kerry is at right.

possibility for a political solution in Syria. Lavrov added that, without Russia, neither the nuclear deal with Iran, nor the agreement for the destruction of the chemical weapons stocks of the Assad government, nor the ceasefire in Syria would have been possible.

What It's Really About

What is it really all about? In an adaptation of the lines of Schiller's poem *Der Antritt des neuen Jahrhunderts* (The Arrival of the New Century) one could say: "Where America vainly wrestles for sole ownership of the world." It's about the desperate attempt to uphold the neo-conservative doctrine of the Project for a New American Century developed by Paul Wolfowitz, Richard Perle, Robert Kagan, and Co.—just at the point at which it has become impossible. This doctrine declares that the United States will not allow any nation or group of nations to challenge its claim to unipolar leadership in the political, economic, or military sphere, plain and simple.

But even this pretension is water under the bridge. China, which is aiming at scientific excellence and advanced technology, has long begun to surpass the trans-Atlantic sector, which clings to the casino economy. While European Central Bank head Mario Draghi prints helicopter money—as the ultimate measure of a bankrupt financial system—China is building high-speed trains and fusion reactors, and launching trailblazing space missions. Which is more "sustainable?" The Chinese model of "win-win" cooperation through the extension of the New Silk Road, and of the infrastructure projects of the "One Belt, One Road" policy, has clearly proved to be the more attractive model. The latest example of the greater attractiveness of the New Silk Road, as opposed to geopolitical confrontation with Russia and China, appeared during the visit of Chinese President Xi Jinping to the Czech Republic. Presidents Xi and Milos Zeman signed off on an extensive list of projects in the areas of high technology, infrastructure, and the real economy, and cele-

This is exactly the intention expressed very clearly by NATO Commander General Philip Breedlove—also known as "Dr. Strangelove"—while he was in Riga, Latvia, April 1 for the announcement of the permanent rotation of 4,200 troops in a U.S. armored brigade starting in 2017: "We are prepared to fight and win if we have to . . . Our focus will expand from assurance to deterrence, including measures that vastly improve our overall readiness." This is necessary, Breedlove said, "as an answer to a resurgent and aggressive Russia." The insinuation that Russia is planning an invasion of the Baltic states is nothing but black propaganda.

To the same category belong the constantly renewed campaign of demonization of Russian President Vladimir Putin and the internationally coordinated campaign against Chinese President Xi Jinping, as well as the shamelessly open campaign of regime change against President Dilma Rousseff in Brazil and President Jacob Zuma in South Africa—all leaders of BRICS countries.

In a refreshing contrast to this war-mongering, U.S. Secretary of State John Kerry, in a joint press conference with Russian Foreign Minister Sergey Lavrov and German Foreign Minister Frank Walter Steinmeier, stressed Russia's positive role in bringing about the

During his trip to several African nations, German Development Minister Gerd Müller emphasized that Europe can only solve the refugee crisis by supporting African economic development. Zepp-LaRouche: "Müller is a small but important exception to the claptrap of European politicians." This is "a baby step in the right direction." Here, Müller visits a refugee camp in South Sudan.

brated the role of the "Golden City" of Prague as the "gateway" for cooperation between China and Europe.

Such collaboration is also the key to the solution of the refugee crisis, which has revealed just how weak the foundations of the European Union (EU) are. China has just announced the appointment of its first special envoy to Syria, Xie Xiaoyan, a former ambassador to Iran, Ethiopia, and the African Union. This gives us justifiable hope that President Xi's offer to extend the New Silk Road into the entire Southwest Asian region—an offer he put on the agenda during his recent trip to Saudi Arabia, Egypt, and Iran—can actually be concretely implemented in the reconstruction of Syria.

Wake Up!

It is high time for German Chancellor Angela Merkel—and the leading institutions of Europe in general—to wake up. The latest political fiasco, of relying on Turkish President Erdogan to deal with the refugee crisis, is just as abhorrent as it is incompetent. All relief organizations, such as Doctors without Borders and the UN Human Rights Commission, are denouncing as inhumane the measures ordered by the EU for the refugees in Greece. Amnesty International has only made public what was already clear: that Erdogan has hoodwinked the EU by pocketing billions on the one side, while sending the refugees back into the war and crisis zones of Syria, Iraq, and Afghani-

stan, a breach of conventions on human rights and refugees.

While Erdogan leads the EU and Chancellor Merkel around by the nose, and at the same time denies the refugees deported from Greece their due protections and puts their lives in danger, the Russian ambassador to the UN has submitted proof to the UN Security Council that Turkey, up to this very day, is sending illegal weapons and military advisers to ISIS in Syria.

What an unbelievable farce is the claptrap of European politicians about common European values, human rights, democracy, and press freedom! And where is the outcry in this holier-than-thou Europe about the more than 2,000 children who have been killed under Saudi bombardments in Yemen? And the more than 300,000 children who are at risk of dying because of undernourishment and the destruction of the health system, both as a result of the Saudi bombing?

German Development Minister Gerd Müller is a small but important exception; during his trip to several African nations he once again emphasized that Europe can only solve the refugee crisis by supporting the economic development of African countries. That is the only way to prevent ever more millions of people from fleeing to Europe to save their lives. A baby step in the right direction.

It is urgent for us in Europe to take a hard look in the mirror and to uncompromisingly realize where we stand. We no longer have any reason to consider ourselves so incredibly superior because of our alleged "European values." Although we not want to believe it, we are becoming the laughing stock of the whole world. Led by the nose by Erdogan, cruel toward the refugees, and a poodle for London and Washington—who are about to pulverize the world on the altar of geopolitics in a thermonuclear war.

Fortunately there is a way out. We can recognize and defend our own interests and, together with China and Russia, stabilize Southwest Asia and Africa through the expansion of the Silk Road into the World Land-Bridge. In that way, we can encourage America to return to its true identity as a republic.

This article, written for the German newspaper Neue Solidarität, *was translated from the German.*

II. Man Discovers Himself

A Unified Mission for the Exploration of Space Is the Pathway to Peace for All Mankind

by Kesha Rogers

"We came in peace for all Mankind"

—Plaque left by the Apollo 11 team on the first Moon landing

March 31—On March 25, 2016, Secretary of State John Kerry gave a press conference with Russian Foreign Minister Sergey Lavrov. Following a series of discussions with Lavrov and President Vladimir Putin, and building on a successful deployment led by President Putin in Syria, Kerry defined the key to what is needed to bring about a permanent cessation of hostilities.

Secretary Kerry described his meeting with American astronaut Scott Kelly, who had just spent more than 340 days in space with his Russian counterpart, Cosmonaut Mikhail Kornienko. Kerry said he had spoken with the two astronauts, one American and one Russian, who were working together on the International Space Station to study the effects of long-term spaceflight on the human body. In his remarks, Kerry presented what he encountered in his meeting with the two astronauts as a critical example of what is required to bring about collaboration in international diplomacy, bringing nations to work together to solve common problems and strengthening our understanding of who we are as human beings.

Can we bring about such collaboration and peace among nations?

The obvious answer is, we can, provided that we act to rid ourselves once and for all of a dying British empire and remove Obama from the Presidency, now. Our U.S. space program, implemented by NASA, must be restored to its rightful place as the spark-plug for a national recovery. This must be done as a key to bringing the United States into collaboration with the nations of Russia and China, along with other nations, thus defining a new paradigm for mankind.

That new paradigm is being demonstrated by China's promotion of the New Silk Road development corridors, its cooperation throughout the world, and its leadership in space exploration, exemplified by the mission to land a rover on the far side of the moon,— embarking on new discoveries, and doing what no nation has yet accomplished. President Obama's attack on NASA's exploration programs has been a complete and utter frontal attack on our nation's future. The question is, how long will you allow this murderous policy to continue?

What Secretary Kerry said is right: The basis for global cooperation among nations in solving the problems we face—from ISIS terrorism to your once-employed neighbor's heroin-induced suicide—should be modeled on the kind of peaceful collaboration that currently exists in certain aspects of the space program. This collaboration must be broadened to join with China's leadership and must embrace all other nations. Countries must actually unite in common cause against the bankrupt British Empire and declare that those brave men and women who pioneered to get the human race beyond Earth a few generations ago, shall not have lived and died in vain. It is time to take the budgetary and political lid off real human progress, and live up to our destiny as mankind in the galaxy.

As a two-time nominee for U.S. Congress in the district representing Johnson Space Center, and later a candidate for U.S. Senate, I have continued to lead the fight against the continued dismantling of the U.S. space program. I hereby call upon the international space community to heed this call for nations to collaborate politically as we do in space, and pull down the barriers to this progress once and for all. That is why I am happy to announce an initiative for an international space policy roundtable on this subject, to be held in Houston, Texas near the Johnson Space Center. I call upon astronauts, scientists, engineers, and policy makers to come together to participate in this indispensable discussion, to determine a unified mission for progress and peaceful relations among nations.

MANHATTAN PROJECT PERFORMS

Handel's *Messiah* on Easter Sunday

by Dennis H. Speed

April 4—The Manhattan Project was first proposed by *EIR* founder Lyndon LaRouche during the preparation of a November, 2014 musical celebration of the birthday of the "poet of freedom," Friedrich Schiller. The Manhattan Project took a major step forward this Easter Sunday, March 27. The Schiller Institute New York City Community Chorus performed Parts Two and Three of *Messiah* by composer George Frideric Handel (1685-1759), in Brooklyn at the Visitation of the Blessed Virgin Mary Roman Catholic Church.

In a discussion the next day among the LaRouche Political Action Committee's Policy Committee, Diane Sare, the chorus co-founder and choral director, reported on the performance of the chorus of the evening before: "This was done at a very important Catholic Church in Brooklyn, which historically was founded in the 1850s, and was the area of longshoreman and port activity, and Italian and Irish immigrants. And we had a full orchestra and chorus, and it's a continuing growth of this choral process that we've been carrying on in Manhattan.

"There were about 400-450 people in attendance, which is saying something because the church as it stands now, is in a semi-industrial area. The church was actually scheduled to be shut down. And the priest made a point at the beginning, when he gave the opening remarks for the event, of speaking a little bit about the history of this church, which is quite beautiful. And he said, 'Can you imagine closing a church which is also a work of art? We couldn't allow that to happen.' And then he described what each of the stained-glass windows was, and the scene of Noah and the Ark, which was very important for a port area. In fact the ceiling of the church is designed to look like the inside of a boat. So it's a beautiful wood arch. And people in the audience were commenting that the acoustics were quite extraordinary, that you could hear every voice perfectly, even at the very back of the church.

Schiller Institute

On Easter Sunday the New York Schiller Institute Community Chorus performed Parts Two and Three of George Frideric Handel's Messiah *at the Visitation of the Blessed Virgin Mary Roman Catholic Church in Brooklyn, New York, March 27, 2016.*

"We had many people who signed up to join the chorus—actually maybe 40 or 50—who expressed immediate interest in immediately joining the chorus that we're organizing in Brooklyn, as a result of this. We discovered that some of the musicians there have collaborated with old friends of LaRouche, like Norbert Brainin (the late first violinist of the great Amadeus Quartet). And it just, again, opens up a whole new potential for what we can do in Manhattan and environs with this choral process."

The Spirit Behind the Music

As reported in the program for the concert, "The church has become well known in New York City in the aftermath of Hurricane Sandy in 2012 for its role in assisting the nearby community during that crisis.... Church pastor Father Claudio Antecini, interviewed by *The Tablet* newspaper three months after the onset of Hurricane Sandy, said of the calamity 'that during times of extreme duress, such as during a hurricane, there is only one thought on many people's minds: How to help others. Visitation Parish helped about 4,000 people from the neighborhood who came looking for food and supplies.' That is the same spirit that characterizes Handel's *Messiah*, first performed in Dublin, Ireland in 1742. Handel demanded and successfully fought to direct that all proceeds from his oratorio's premiere should go to benefit the cities' debtors' prisons, the Mercers' Hospital, and the Charitable Infirmary."

Policy Committee member Rachel Brinkley, who had sung in the chorus of the Sunday event, responded to Sare: "It was very interesting to actually perform the end of Handel's *Messiah*. I didn't know, or I never quite understood the piece as a whole. But generally, this idea of splitting it up gets rid of the section at the end, and Handel's composition of this particular piece really, I think, did intend for people to stay through to the end. Not just stand up and leave at the 'Hallelujah' chorus; that's beautiful, the 'Hallelujah.' But the end, which ends with 'Amen.' and the principle of immortality, is much more important, when it says, 'The trumpet shall sound, the dead shall be raised incorruptible, and we shall be changed. For this corruptible must put on incorruption, and this mortal must put on immortality.' And this particular performance, I thought, had a clear dialogue between the soloist and the chorus, echoing and producing these changes between mortality and immortality. So, it was very beautiful.

"And then also, the question of Handel's connection to Leibniz was also something that I wasn't aware of before this performance. But it turns out that Handel was sent to London, essentially by Leibniz. He was hired by the court at Hanover and sent to London, to be a liaison between Queen Anne and Sophie in Hanover. So, Handel went to London with the idea of bringing Leibniz's ideas there, and his composition of *Messiah* was after the death of Princess Caroline, whom he had worked with, who was Leibniz's student. And he was inspired by his work with her, and wrote this piece. So it was definitely a work for history to be performing this right now."

There is a Classical cultural method being applied to attack the madness of the present state of American society in these actions. The Schiller Institute New York City Community Chorus was founded in December 2014 with a sing-along performance of Handel's *Messiah* dedicated to unifying the city of New York in the wake of the Staten Island grand jury decision in the suffocation death of Eric Garner. Just over a year later, and in this Easter celebration, there were more than 100 performers, including a 31-piece orchestra and 80 singers led by conductor John Sigerson, the Music Director of the Schiller Institute.

Sigerson is the co-author of the groundbreaking work, *A Manual On Registration and Tuning*, published by the Schiller Institute in 1988. He is the nation's leading proponent of orchestral performance at the Verdi tuning of A=432 cycles per second, significantly lower than the tuning practice of most major orchestras in Europe and the United States.

Sigerson's conducting of *Messiah* is heavily influenced by his studies of the work of conductor Wilhelm Furtwängler, one of history's greatest musicians, and the greatest conductor of the Twentieth Century. In discussion the next day, Sigerson suggested that people listen to Furtwängler performances of Handel's *Concerti Grossi* to gain a more introspective insight into the highest quality of Handel's compositional method, the which is sometimes missed because of the tendency to think of Handel as merely a "festive" composer. It was the attempt to present *Messiah* as one singular idea, as opposed to a collection of "greatest hits," that was the distinction of the performance.

Soloists Gudrun Bühler (soprano), Mary Phillips (mezzo-soprano), Everett Suttle (tenor), and Phillip Cutlip (bass) allowed the long-line intent to be punctuated by drama, fire, and reflection through Handel's arias. More work is required on the recitative/aria rela-

Schiller Institute

Gudrun Bühler, soprano

Schiller Institute

Philip Cutlip, bass-baritone

tionship and its realization between symphony, soloist, and chorus.

Maybe It's the Tuning

Of the chorus itself, Sigerson reported a conversation between himself and another musician who remarked on their exceptional singing. "He was amazed—he sings in other choruses in New York City—how well our chorus stays in tune! In all the other choruses everybody's going flat! [I said to him] 'Maybe it's the tuning; also we strive for *bel canto* and not pushing the voice.' [Then he asked me] 'Do you need an assistant?'"

The conclusion of the piece, "Worthy Is the Lamb," followed by "Amen," an intricate fugue and one of Handel's greatest compositional moments, lifts the chorus to the level of single soloist. While many of the choruses of *Messiah* are impressive, the concluding "Amen," precisely because of the absence of text, other than that one word of simultaneous submission, celebration, and recognition of universal law, is the most liberating moment of the piece, which is best experienced as a whole. Sigerson announced at the end of the discussion on Monday that he believed that the chorus should perform the whole of *Messiah*, all three sections, at the end of the year. Whole *Messiah* performances, while done, are quite rare; a *Messiah* done at the proper "Verdi tuning" is generally unavailable to the public, and would almost never be done for the non-"professional concert-going" audiences of New York City that Sare, Sigerson, and the New York City Community Chorus seek to reach.

These performances aim to rejoin a campaign for cultural literacy and true cultural freedom that was taken up in New York City nearly three decades ago. As the Easter program reported, "On April 9, 1988, at a conference on 'Music and Classical Aesthetics' at the Casa di Verdi in Milan, Italy, the Schiller Institute launched a worldwide campaign to restore the scientific tuning pitch of the Classical composers from Bach through Verdi, of Middle C=256 Hz ('A' no higher than 432 Hz).

"Five years later, on April 8, 1993, the famous Italian tenor Carlo Bergonzi, a participant at the earlier conference (which included Lyndon and [Schiller Institutes founder] Helga LaRouche, as well as Italian opera luminaries soprano Renata Tebaldi and baritone Piero Capuccilli) established, in a seminar held at Carnegie's Weill Recital Hall, the superiority, through demonstrations with male and female singers, of the Verdi tuning over the arbitrarily high 'modern' tuning of A=440 Hz, and even higher. Bergonzi stated, 'It is particularly important to raise the question of tuning in connection with *bel canto* technique, since today's high tuning misplaces all register shifts, and makes it very difficult for a singer to have the sound float above the breath. When an F-sharp becomes a G... Everything is misplaced a half-step, and the technique fails.'"

It was Lyndon LaRouche who insisted to colleagues over thirty years ago that the advancement of music, or even the preservation of Classical compositional method, required the restoration of the "human tuning" system of C=256. In 1990, conductor Anthony Morss conducted a concert opera version of Beethoven's *Fidelio* at the proper tuning, nearly three years before the Bergonzi interview. Maestro Morss recently retired

Mary Phillips, mezzo-soprano, and Everett Suttle, tenor, singing the duet: "O death, where is thy sting?" (1 Corinthians 15:55-56).

Schiller Institute

October 2014, Lyndon La-Rouche launched his 'Manhattan Project,' of which this chorus is a part. LaRouche maintained that the legacy of Alexander Hamilton and of his extraordinary efforts, *from Manhattan*, to unify our young nation through the American Revolution and the American System of economy based on the creativity of our citizens, is the crucial source of identity of the United States." It is to the idea of the reproduction of great ideas for all of humanity through establishing a *unity of effect*—whether in politics, art, or science—that the chorus is devoted.

from directing two orchestras in New Jersey, having conducted for over 55 years throughout the world, and accompanied soprano Joan Sutherland and others of the world's greatest singers.

Since retiring last year, Maestro Morss has been a member of the New York City Community Chorus and sings in the bass section. The chorus's accompanist, pianist/harpsichordist Cheryl Berard, is an accomplished recitalist in her own right. These and others of the best musicians in New York stand and sit side by side with people who have often only recently began to sing,— yet who, through a shared mission to impart beauty to an America marred by the ugliness of the madness of its politics, produced a *Messiah* that was not merely competent, but in some instances inspired.

The concert notes describing the Schiller Institute chorus, written by Diane Sare, explain why this is possible. "The question of 'our humanity' is the most important question facing the American population today. If you were to presume that the current pack of Presidential candidates and the quality of their debates were representative of 'humanity,' you might place an urgent call to China and request to board the nearest spacecraft in search of superior species in some other galaxy!"

Unity of Effect

Sare continued, "Happily, it is the view of Friedrich Schiller that such low points in our history do not define our species, but that we are capable of better, and that the role of the artist is to inspire us to act in a truly human, as distinct from bestial, manner. It is to this end that in

In his Saturday dialogue with the Manhattan Project held at the Beacon Hotel after the concert, Lyndon La-Rouche was asked a question by a participant in Sunday's concert, who contended that he thought that the performance had a resonating effect in the thinking and organizing of all those that experienced it. Part of the question was stated: "...I know in your book, *The Science of Christian Economy*, you talk about how it takes creativity to make an original, valid, scientific discovery, but also, to transmit that to others, you need a certain level of creativity. And essentially what we're doing or discussing here today [the removal of Obama from office through impeachment], is to do the impossible. But if you really think about it, it's actually very simple; it's just that people *think* that it's impossible, and they act on that belief. And I think that if we were consistently operating on the same level of creativity that we did … expressed in this concert, we would easily win. So my question is, where does this level of creativity really come from? And how can we, as a group, have more of that?"

LaRouche replied: "There are many answers to that question. The Italian answer is probably one of the best answers of all. I spent a good deal, a quarter of my time in Europe, in particular, with Italian figures. Some of them were musicians, and people like that, so I had a lot of Italian friends, and most of the Italian friends would fit in the same category as the people who performed at the recent event there.

"The people are drawn to that because intrinsically

in the religious service, there's an implicit direction,—and never underrate implicit direction. Implicit direction, which most people, you know, where they sing religious songs, most of them don't know what they are doing. They have an understanding about it. They have a reason why they are impressed by this. They enjoy this. They have a certain sense of comfort. And I think the greatest things in religious behavior that you would get from those locations, are just exactly that.

"They don't know what they are adapting to. They don't know fully what the purpose of their action is, but they get a resonance of something there which is bigger than they are! And they sing for the sake of singing for something which is bigger than they are.

"And what happened in that particular case, and the one earlier last year [December 19-20], was the same thing. Why do people go into these religious formalities in these things? Because they are seeking to find *home*. They're seeking to find the experience of life which they can call their *immortal home*. That's what they want. And when you can give them that, or suggest how they could do that, they're happy.

"The usual stuff about religion—most people who are religious don't know anything about what religion is. They get a grab at it; they get something, a feeling

about it. But what it's really about is the devotion of a human being's *life*: The meaning of the life of any human being, is what does the life of that human being contribute to the benefit of mankind, *permanently*?

"Mankind, all human beings die. Children die. The greatest children have outlived their parents, and what they became gave us the richness of what that child had accomplished.

"So there's a process in mankind, where the action of mankind under certain conditions actually promotes and insists upon an improvement into what mankind *will be*, in the course of their life, the *meaning* of their life. Can you say, 'Well I'm going to be successful, I'm going to get money, I'm going to get this, I'm going to…,'—is that going to make a difference for you? If you're going to *die*, will that make a difference for you?

"Or if you could live a life which can mean something, and when you can discover things in yourself which are creative and great, you may not understand why you are doing that, but you experience that, and therefore you say, 'I'm not going to go against it. This is something I don't fully understand. I believe in it, but I don't fully understand it. And I would hope that my children will understand that better.'

"And that's what this thing was about."

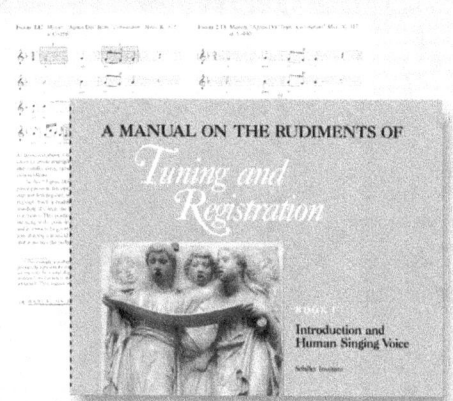

Ionization: The Power of a Weak Force to Water the Earth

by Benjamin Deniston

March 28—Understanding the implications of living within our Galaxy provides new insights for the management of the Earth's water system.[1] Over the past decades, as *EIR* has reported, teams of scientists and engineers in several countries have developed relatively small, affordable systems of thin, high-voltage wires (supported by towers or other structures) to manage and increase precipitation by controlling the ionization levels of the local atmosphere.

One company, Australian Rain Technologies (ART), has just released details of its third successful year in its ongoing five-year trial in Oman. This Oman trial follows four successful trials in two locations in Australia from 2007 to 2010.[2]

The general ART approach is similar to other operations, including ELAT (*Electrificación Local de la Atmósfera Terrestre SA*) systems that have been used for commercial operations in Mexico and Israel.[3] Some of the details of these operations were brought to our attention by the Russian scientist Sergey Pulinets, who was part of an independent scientific team brought in to evaluate the operations in Mexico.[4]

Although it is not usually discussed by the proponents of these ionization systems, understanding these systems can help provide insights into how our Galaxy

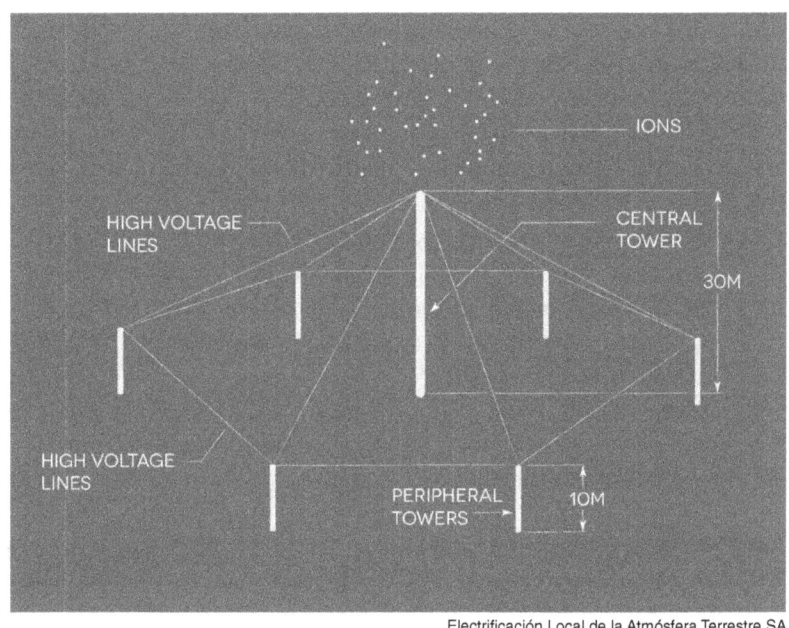

Electrificación Local de la Atmósfera Terrestre SA

The design of the ELAT atmospheric ionization systems used in Mexico. The towers support high-voltage lines that generate negatively charged ions in the atmosphere.

controls key aspects of the Earth's water, weather, and climate systems. When understood from this standpoint, we recognize that these ionization systems provide a potential to manage the global water cycle from a galactic perspective.

Living in the Galaxy

Galactic cosmic radiation, in net energy terms a relatively *weak force*, permeates the Earth's atmosphere, providing the dominant source of ionization throughout much of the atmosphere. These galactic ionization levels, in turn, have significant effects on the rate of condensation of water vapor, the formation of clouds, and related processes, leading to the following effects:

Short-term variations (days to weeks) in this galactic ionization can affect some of the most powerful

---

1. "Memo for the Next President: New Perspectives on the Western Water Crisis," https://larouchepac.com/sites/default/files/20150330-Water%20Crisis.pdf

2. See http://www.australianrain.com.au

3. For more background, see a review of these technologies in "Atmospheric Moisture Control," http://www.larouchepub.com/eiw/public/2015/ eirv42n16-20150417/18-25_4216.pdf

4. See the May 2015 LaRouche PAC interview with Professor Pulinets, "End Droughts with Weather Control," https://www.youtube.com/watch?v=0iKFTlphuJs

weather systems (under the right conditions).[5] These variations are generally produced by sudden, explosive outbursts of plasma from the Sun (carrying magnetic fields that temporarily shield Earth from some of the galactic cosmic radiation as the plasma bursts pass by.

• Medium-term variations (years to centuries) drive climate change by modulating low-level cloud cover.[6] These variations are generally produced by cycles of solar activity.

• Very long term variations (over millions of years) are responsible for the largest and most persistent changes in the Earth's climate system.[7] These variations are produced by changes in our Galactic environment as the Solar System travels through the Galaxy, and by changes in the activity of the galactic systems as a whole.

Thus, ionization levels—whether natural (galactic) or controlled by man—are key to the behavior of the critical atmospheric phase of the Earth's water cycle.

New Results from Oman

At the 2016 International Water Conference in Muscat, Oman, ART announced that the third year of its five-year trial continued to show successful results. Over its initial three years of operation, the Oman trial has provided an 18% increase in rainfall in the area of ionization. This assessment is based on data provided by new weather stations and a few hundred rain gauges (placed inside and outside of the target area), providing the information needed to accurately estimate what the rainfall would have been under natural conditions (i.e., without the enhancement provided by the ionization systems). Independent evaluations of these results are provided by the National Institute for Applied Statistical Research Australia at the University of Wollongong.

Rainfall Enhancement with the Atlant

Australian Rain Technologies

The rainfall enhancement process is shown here to illustrate the Atlant system of Australian Rain Technologies. The tower is at the bottom center in yellow. The system generates negatively charged ions that attach themselves, by virtue of their charge, to particles in the atmosphere (aerosols). The particles become "seeds" for the condensation of water vapor. The system depends on the presence of water vapor in the atmosphere, hence the expression, "rain enhancement."

Australian Rain Technologies

A rain enhancement system built by Australian Rain Technologies in Australia.

For a better insight into the significance of these results, let's examine the details for 2014.

In 2014 ART operated four ionization stations for 140 days, *enhancing rainfall by 33% over a 16,000 square-kilometer area.* It estimates that this amounted to 96 million cubic meters of additional surface water flow. The four ionization stations ran at 500 watts each, so (assuming they all ran the entire time) only 2 kilowatts of power was needed to power the entire ionization process.

5. V.G. Bondur, S.A. Pulinets, and G.A. Kim, "The Role of Galactic Cosmic Rays in Tropical Cyclogenesis: Evidence of Hurricane Katrina," *Doklady Earth Sciences,* 2008, Vol. 422, No. 2, pp. 244-249.
6. H. Svensmark and E. Friis-Christensen, "Reply to Lockwood and Fröhlich: The persistent role of the Sun in climate forcing," Danish National Space Center Scientific Research Report 3/2007.
7. Nir J. Shaviv, "The spiral structure of the Milky Way, cosmic rays, and ice age epochs on Earth," *New Astronomy,* Volume 8, Issue 1, Jan. 2003, pp. 39-77.

Tex Whitney Productions

The placement of the towers in the Australian Rain Technologies trial in Oman.

One last consideration provides additional insights into the significance of living within our Galaxy.

Latent Heat and Galactic Cosmic Rays

Since the condensation of water vapor releases the same amount of energy (latent heat) that was required to initially evaporate that water (energy originally provided by the Sun), we can also determine that the energy equivalent of 50 megatons of TNT was released by the condensation of this 96 million cubic meters of water (while this is a lot of energy, it was dispersed over a large area and over a long time period). Recognizing this, we can draw the following conclusions about the energetics of the process:

• Over 140 days of operation, an average of 18 gigawatts of power was being released in the form of latent heat.

• Over the 16,000 square-kilometer area, this comes to an average of 1.1 watts per square meter.

• Two kilowatts of power input can trigger the release of nine million times as much power, 18 billion watts (18 gigawatts)!

This brings us back to the role of the Galaxy in controlling processes on Earth. While the net total energy of Galactic cosmic rays is relatively low, its qualitative effect, via the ionization process, can be very substantial.

Even on very short time scales, the modulation of latent heat release via an ionization system such as the one described here, shows how variations in the relatively low energy input of Galactic cosmic rays can affect the severity of incredibly powerful weather systems, such as hurricanes and cyclones, as Sergey Pulinets and his associates have already shown.[8]

At the other extreme, Nir Shaviv and Henrik Svensmark have shown that the Galaxy controls the largest and most sustained variations in the Earth's climate, on a scale of tens and hundreds of millions of years.

Mankind is coming to actively understand our cosmic-galactic environment and is learning to manage that environment for our betterment.

Using two kilowatts of power for 140 days to generate 96 million cubic meters of additional fresh water amounts to an average production of 680,000 cubic meters (180 million gallons) per day, and an average energy productivity of 14,000 cubic meters (3.7 million gallons) of fresh water produced per kilowatt-hour.

From this we can make the following comparison with another method for increasing freshwater availability, desalination.

Ionization vs Desalination: Fresh Water per Unit Energy

For comparison, the Carlsbad desalination plant in southern California, currently among the most efficient in the world, provides only 0.3 cubic meters (80 gallons) per kilowatt-hour—which means that in 2014, the ionization systems in Oman produced 50,000 times more water per unit of energy!

The average rate of total freshwater generated was similar in both cases. The Carlsbad desalination plant is producing 50 million gallons per day, while the Oman ionization trial in 2014 generated an average of 180 million gallons per day over the 140 days of operation (or 70 million gallons per day, if averaged over an entire year).

The increased surface water flow from ionization is obviously much more dispersed than the output from a desalination plant, and not all of it can be collected for use. However, ionization systems can be used to direct increased precipitation into watersheds that feed into existing water management infrastructure, as was done in Mexico and Israel, capturing much of it for economic use.

---

8. V.G. Bondur, S.A. Pulinets, and G.A. Kim, "The Role of Galactic Cosmic Rays in Tropical Cyclogenesis: Evidence of Hurricane Katrina," *Doklady Earth Sciences,* 2008, Vol. 422, No. 2, pp. 244-249.

III. The New Silk Road

THE CHINA-PAKISTAN ECONOMIC CORRIDOR

Pakistan's Cornucopia in Waiting

by Ramtanu Maitra

April 4—There are many aspects of the China-Pakistan Economic Corridor (CPEC), when completed, which will enable Pakistan to launch an overall nation-wide development perspective. Pakistan's biggest shortcomings after almost 70 years of its existence have been its inability to carry out even nominal development of its western and southern parts constituting the Northern Area, Khyber-Pakhtoonkhwa, and Balochistan provinces. Much of Sindh province's rural areas have also undergone little agro-industrial development during this period.

The CPEC plans to change all that. The plan centers around two major ingredients: building power plants and developing connectivity. Once these are accomplished, Pakistan will be ready to develop its agro-industrial capabilities. A few additional ingredients will be required during the interim period, including building up a pool of skilled workers.

Expansion of Power Infrastructure

Pakistan is a power-starved nation. According to the United States Institute of Peace (USIP) report in 2015, Pakistan is currently facing a severe and multifaceted energy crisis. Electricity shortages exceeded 7,000 megawatts in 2011, and the gas shortfall is 2 billion cubic feet per day. The energy shortages are estimated to cost around two percent of GDP annually.

This shortfall is the result of the failure, over successive governments' tenures, to invest enough to expand power system capacity. Low and declining investment and savings rates (including in power) reflect macroeconomic weaknesses.[1]

In reality, however, the shortfall is much more severe. The country's overall capacity of power generation (but not the peak power supply, which is about 60% of generation capacity in the best of times) is 23,538 MW, leaving a shortfall of nearly 40,000 to 60,000 MW. According to Pakistan's Water and Power Development Authority (WAPDA), national power demand at levels of peak demand will reach 40,000 MW by 2020.

CPEC addresses this problem directly. Under CPEC, China will invest $33.8 billion in thermal, nuclear, solar, and wind power generation facilities and projects to overcome Pakistan's energy shortages. The completion of these project during the 15 years of CPEC development will ensure the country's economic growth with tangible economic benefits that will be derived from its subsequent agro-industrial developments. Although all the power projects have been not been cleared yet, the following projects, showing a province-wide breakdown, have been named as of now:

In Sindh (10,250 MW):
- Port Qasim Coal Power Plant 2,270 MW,
- Thar Coal Power Plant 3,300 MW,
- Jamshoro Power Project 1,320 MW,
- Wind Power Projects 500 MW,
- Nuclear Power Plants 2,200 MW,
- Lakhra Coal Power Plant 660 MW.

In Khyber Pakhtoonkhwa (8,230 MW):
- Sukki Kinari Hydro Power Station 870 MW,
- Dasu Hydro Power Project 4,320 MW,
- Tarbela IV & V Extension 2,700 MW,
- Alai Khawar Hydro Power Project 121 MW,
- Khan Khawar Hydro Power Project 72 MW,
- Dabeer Khawar Hydro Power Project 130 MW,
- Gomalzam Hydro Power Project 17 MW.

In Azad Kashmir—the Pakistan-held part of the disputed state of Jammu and Kashmir (4,029 MW):
- Neelam Jehlum Project 979 MW,
- Karot Hydro Power Project 720 MW,
- Kohala Hydro Power Project 1,100MW,
- Mehl Hydro Power Project 590 MW,
- Azad Pattan Hydro Power Project 640 MW.

In Balochistan (4,200 MW):
- Hubco Coal Power Project 3,600 MW,
- Gwadar Coal Power Project 600 MW.

---

1. Rashid Aziz and Munawar Baseer Ahmad, *Pakistan's Power Crisis: The Way Forward*, USIP Special Report 375, June 2015.

In Punjab (6,220 MW):
- Coal Power Plants (Sahiwal and Salt Range) 1,620 MW,
- Quaid-e-Azam Solar Park 1,000 MW,
- RLNG-based plants 3,600 MW.

In Gilgit Baltistan, also part of disputed state of Jammu and Kashmir (11,917):
- Diamer Bhasha Hydro Power Project 4,800,
- Bonji Hydro Power Project 7,100 MW,
- Satpara Hydro Power Project 17 MW.

Completion of these projects will add more than 44,000 MW to Pakistan's generation capacity. In addition, CPEC also includes building some transmission lines to connect the power generation source to Pakistan's power grid.

Crucial Transport Infrastructure

The second aspect of the CPEC which will significantly open up economic development prospects in Pakistan is the connectivity the project will provide. The connectivity within Pakistan is an important element not only for Pakistan's future development but to ensure the blossoming of a network of trade routes among China, Pakistan, Central Asia, and Iran—by land and through Gwadar Port by sea.

Since the CPEC's prime objective is to enter Pakistan in the north through Khunjerab Pass into Gilgit-Baltistan and move southward to Balochistan's Gwadar Port, winding its way through northern Punjab, Khyber Pakhtoonkhwa, and Balochistan, priority has been given to building a 392 km motorway between Sukkur in Sindh province in the south and Multan in Punjab province in the north. Recently, China State Construction Engineering Corporation (CSCEC) signed a $2.89 billion contract to officially launch the construction of the motorway which is expected to improve transport conditions of the most populous and developed regions in Pakistan. This stretch of the motorway, when constructed, will become part of the much longer Karachi-to-Peshawar motorway, a key part of the CPEC.

In addition, two other motorways to facilitate the development of CPEC have been envisaged. One is planned to pass through central Pakistan and the other through eastern Pakistan, linking such major cities as Faisalabad and Lahore.

CPEC includes plans to upgrade Pakistan's now-rickety railroads. The identified sections include a new railway track from Gwadar to Quetta and Jacobabad via Besima—all located in Pakistan's southwestern Balochistan province. In addition, some 560 km of railway track will be laid from Bostan, north of Quetta, to Kotla Jam in Punjab, via Zhob and Dera Ismail Khan in Khyber Pakhtoonkhwa, while 682 km of track will be laid from Havelian, south of Abbottabad in Punjab, to Khunjrab on the China-Pakistan border on the way to Kashgar in China's Xinjiang province.

Also on the agenda is an upgrade of 1,872 km of railway track from Karachi to Peshawar via Kotri, Multan, Lahore, and Rawalpindi, and some 1,254 km of railway track from Kotri in Sindh to Attock City—in Punjab close to Islamabad—via Dadu, Larkana, Jacobabad, Der Ghazi Khan, Bhakkar, and Kundian.

An established connectivity with China, and within Pakistan, and enhancement of Pakistan's power generation capacity will open up opportunities for Islamabad to develop big agro-industrial economic corridors. That success, in the not so distant future, will enable Pakistan to connect itself with neighboring nations to further brighten its economic future.

To be continued Part 3: CPEC: The challenges in developing the route.

Arabic Land-Bridge Report Printed in Yemen

April 14—On March 23, 2016—simultaneous with the EIR-sponsored Frankfurt conference "Solving the Economic and Refugee Crises with the New Silk Road!"[1] —Fouad al-Ghaffari, a friend of the LaRouche Movement, released the Arabic-language translation of *The New Silk Road Becomes the World Land-Bridge* report in Sana'a, the capital city of Yemen.

Frankfurt seminar participant Hussein Askary sent a video message to the Sana'a, Yemen event.

In releasing the report al-Ghaffari issued both a personal greeting and an official press release. Excerpts follow:

The Greeting

"Dr. Abdul Aziz al-Magaleh,[2] today in the celebration of the advisory office for coordination with BRICS and from the Yemeni Center for Studies and Research, announces the launching of the reading of the Arabic report, *The New Silk Road Becomes the World Land-Bridge,* in the republic of Yemen, and expresses the report as an objective report that extends bridges to the countries in the third world which are suffering enormous misery and suffering. He also confirmed that we are addressing an international event made by great and experienced minds through long expertise, and called for moving the waters to build the nation by the intellectuals."

Press Release

"In the presence and sponsorship of Dr. Abdul Aziz al-Magaleh, the Chairman of the Yemeni Center for

Dr. Abdul Aziz al-Magaleh (left) and Fouad al-Ghaffari (center) at a press conference in Sana'a, Yemen, on March 23, as they announced the release of the Arabic-language translation of The New Silk Road Becomes the World Land-Bridge.

Studies and Research, the advisory office for coordination with BRICS, Al Fouad Solutions launched today, the 23rd of March 2016, the program of reading the Arabic report, *The New Silk Road Becomes the World Land Bridge.*

"The first session is supported by the Chairman of the advisory body of the office and occurs in the presence of a number of intellectuals, academics, media, businessmen and businesswomen, and bankers.

"The best introduction of the report was made by the translator of the report, intellectual Hussein Askary. The report was made by a group of intellectuals, working for a period of forty years, headed by a German lady, Mrs. Helga LaRouche, the Chairman of Schiller Institute, widely known as the Lady of the New Silk Road for her leadership in presenting the project of the New Silk Road to the BRICS countries.

"This report is considered as an educational refer-

---

1. For a report on the conference, see *EIR, April 1, 2016*.
2. A poet and former President of Sana'a University, and now the Head of the Center for Studies and Research in Yemen.

ence that sums up the great experiences of various nations, including similar experiences of the Arab World today, which have enabled them to build a better future for their nations.

"This report also shows the experiences of nations that started building their economy and civilization in the right way but faced certain deteriorations, and this led them to change their way of thinking and provoked the people and the leaders to go back to ground zero.

"The report launched today in Yemen, after being officially launched in Egypt on March 7, 2016, is a great description of the nature of the new international system that started with the establishment of the BRICS, and the announcement by China of its intention to cooperate with all the countries worldwide to build the economic belt for the New Silk Road.

"The advisory office for coordination with the BRICS is seeking a new way of thinking to pay tribute to the martyrs and the wounded people on all fighting fronts and to be able to prepare the decision makers to end this vicious death cycle and create an economy based on production and not on austerity measures—to present hope to the people in the right time.

"The office considers the BRICS philosophies as free dynamics to a new system of international relations made by the five fast growing nations worldwide (Brazil, Russia, India, China, South Africa) which was born as the new modern genius to represent a life boat to save humanity from the floods of the collapse of the world Imperial System that has involved the world in a series of conflicts and wars.

"The advisory office believes that Yemen's problem is not the lack of money, but it is the lack of *vision*. Hence we should adopt the vision that would have the faith of the people to defend it, and act to fulfill the outcomes of the national dialogue conference and the agreement that peace and partnership must be the main solution, after trying other solutions hundreds of times. The economic change to be made is the one that would make the world look to Yemen as an opportunity, not as a burden.

"At the end of the workshop, the advisory office for coordination with BRICS is grateful to the Yemeni Center for Studies and Research for sponsoring the program of reading the report every Tuesday, and the office is expressing thanks and appreciation for all who supported them to reach this advanced stage.

"The advisory office for coordination with BRICS is exerting its best efforts, along with a wide spectrum from the government side, civil society, private sector and mixed-sector businessmen, and it has taken executive steps to reach its goals:

• Raising a proposal on the importance of forming a National Committee for Coordination with BRICS.

• Reaching out to the World Club of the Youth on the BRICS.

• Adopting the proposal of forming an operations room for the preparation of a Bank of Reconstruction and inviting external experts to design the bank, which is a demanding requirement, to solve the problems of money and internally displaced persons together.

• Reading the first Chinese Policy Document for the Arab Nation and arranging for its translation with the concerned community partners, due to the importance of this document in drawing the new line of Chinese International Relations.

• Raising the proposal of forming an economic delegation to travel to see the economic indications of the new economic system.

• Reading the New Silk Road book, according to the program here, every Tuesday—to expose the reality and to show the benefits Yemen will get from the passage of the New Silk Road.

• Adding the discussion of Yemen to the second edition of the New Silk Road Report."

Hope in the Midst of Hell

One year ago, in March 2015, Saudi Arabia, acting as a proxy for the Obama Administration and the British Empire, began a sustained terror campaign of air warfare against the nation of Yemen. The Saudi air strikes, which continue to this day, have been indiscriminate, utilizing cluster and other banned anti-personal bombs to hit schools, hospitals, markets, private homes, centers for the blind and disabled, and other humanitarian targets. According to UNICEF, at least six children have been killed or maimed in the fighting every day for the past year, and this represents only the verified casualties, with UNICEF stating that the actual totals are almost certainly much higher.

One week before the March 22, 2016 Brussels terrorist attacks, a Saudi-led air strike bombed a market in Mastaba, Yemen. Although more people died in Mastaba than in Brussels—106 versus 34—the media and the international community in general ignored that earlier atrocity, as they have ignored most of the 150 indiscriminate aerial attacks reported by the United Nations during the last year.

Almost all of the military hardware, including the planes, bombs, and logistical support utilized by Saudi government in this air war of terror has come from either the United States or Great Britain. Saudi Arabia is now the world's largest purchaser of weapons, and in 2015 it purchased $20 billion worth of weapons from the United States and over $4 billion from Britain. The United Arab Emirates, Saudi Arabia's main partner in the Yemen war, is now the world's fourth-largest purchaser of weapons, acquiring $1.07 billion from the U.S. and $65.5 million from Britain last year.

The situation inside Yemen is a genocidal catastrophe. In addition to the more than 6,500 civilians killed and 30,000 wounded, the nation is under almost complete embargo. More than 600 health centers have shut as medicine and other supplies have disappeared. In August 2015, the head of the International Red Cross stated, "Yemen after five months looks like Syria after five years," and in terms of the "numbers of people in need" the humanitarian crisis in Yemen was "the largest in the world," according to the UN Security Council.

Out of Yemen's total population of 24 million, it is estimated that 21 million now require urgent aid, that 18 million lack access to safe clean water, and that more than half lack access to food. UNICEF officials in Yemen state that there are more than 850,000 half-starved children in the country, and outright starvation is now killing increasing numbers. UNICEF also estimates that in the last twelve months the number of children who died from preventable diseases increased by 10,000 over the previous twelve-month period.

Fighting for a Future

At the March 23rd event in Sana'a, Yemen, where the Arabic-language translation of *The New Silk Road Becomes the World Land-Bridge* was released, Fouad al-Ghaffari announced that this meeting would be followed up by readings from the Land-Bridge Report, to be held on a weekly basis.

The first of these readings took place on March 29, and in a report from that meeting Hussein Askary had the following to say:

"An indication of the shift taking place in the world is that in Yemen, *people being bombarded by the old order are meeting to read the materials of the new order!* There were five more writers and poets at the second reading than the first.

"Look at what we have achieved! We are not telling people good news; we are not frightening people with bad news, and then giving them good news to make them feel better. We are creating a new geometry in the world—with Russia, China, and others. We have to get people away from this idea of the British order as having so much money, so much media power. They are wrong. *There is a new dynamic in the world and we are providing the ideas for that dynamic.* We must convey to our supporters that we are changing the world. They should turn their TVs off and stop listening to the commentators who were wrong about the economy, wrong about Syria, wrong about everything. We must convey to people that we are operating in a new geometry."

Another report on the same meeting was forwarded from Fouad al-Ghaffari, in which he stated the following:

"In the second session of the program of reading the Arabic report, *The New Silk Road Becomes the World Land-Bridge,* and after the successful unique launching by Dr. Abdul Aziz al-Magaleh on March 23, the advisor office for coordination with BRICS held its activity today, March 29, 2016, sponsored by the Yemeni Youth Businessmen & Women Committee, which attended the session for the reading of the first and second chapters, read by intellectuals Mr. Faiz al-Bokhary, Mr. Abdulbasit al-Mashwaly, and Mr. Zaid Alfagayh.

"At the opening of the session, Advisor Fouad al-Ghaffari welcomed all the attendees including intellectuals, businessmen, poets, and economic figures, as the right and healthy trend since the start of reading the report.

"He confirmed the importance of implementing the UN Security Council Resolution No. 2250, about youth, in accordance with what is believed in the *New Silk Road* report as a practical guide to the World Land-Bridge for the Yemeni young businessmen and businesswomen.

"Mr. Hareth al-Zubairi, the Deputy of Yemeni Youth Business Committee, delivered a speech expressing the need to cope with change and the need to seize the opportunity available, praising highly the cooperation with the team of advisory cooperation with BRICS.

"Today's meeting was presented by Ms. Fatima Abu Dyna, and the discussions were facilitated by Mr. Mohammed al-Nunu, the Executive Manager of the Advisory Council.

"The session had various discussions and inquiries and advices about the new international land-bridge...."

In Memoriam

Donald Phau

March 28—Donald Phau, a gentle poetic man, an intrepid political organizer, a creative and original historical investigator, passed away March 16 at the age of 66 from complications of advanced-stage Multiple Sclerosis.

In his life Don suffered overwhelming trials and hardships, maintaining his idealism and his optimism throughout, until his disease won out.

He was born in New York in 1950, the son of Benjamin Phau, a television repair expert and master builder of model ships, and Frances Phau, a homemaker of inspiring, sharp intellect. Don was a "gadget" boy who like his father saw into the logic of things mechanical and electronic. He attended the Bronx High School of Science, an elite public school.

While attending the New York State University at Stony Brook, Don encountered and soon joined the political movement associated with Lyndon LaRouche. In that association he found his wings, as a political fighter and original thinker.

During the early 1970s in New York City, Don figured in an incident that led to significant changes in a segment of the American political scene. He was distributing the movement's *New Solidarity* newspaper, which attacked the City's slavemaster-like use of jobless poor people as low-wage replacements for employed labor, as a design to promote racism and break unions. He was assaulted in the street by purported members of the Communist Party, and his nose was broken. In the ensuing political conflict, the revelation that some 50% of the members of that party were FBI agents or dupes, helped bring about a revulsion among intelligent Americans against the New Left in which the Communist Party had become enmeshed.

Don moved for a time to France as an organizer. He gained original insights into the global role of Lafayette, which bore fruit in his writings (on both Lafayette and Beethoven), and in Don's consultation with others.

In 1980 *Campaigner* magazine published Don's devastating reassessment of the republic's founding,

Courtesy of Deborah Sonnenblick
Donald Phau (1950-2016)

"The Treachery of Thomas Jefferson." He demonstrated that Jefferson, as American ambassador to France, had worked with British East India Company intriguers in France to develop fake radical currents hostile to the American Revolution and to the American-French alliance. He showed that Jefferson carried this covert and malicious role back to the United States, and it was as a pro-feudal British Free Trade proponent that Jefferson led the southern slave-owners who fought against Alexander Hamilton's program for high-wage, modern industry.

Don's groundbreaking 1982 article, "How Benjamin Franklin Organized American Industrial Growth," appeared in *EIR*. It conveyed Don's discovery, that it was as an old man that the Revolutionary War leader and scientist Franklin personally organized the cadres and the programs that made economic nationalism and scientific progress the Federal Republic's founding mission.

Don became a defendant in the Wall Street establishment's use of the federal government for a witch-hunt against the LaRouche movement in the 1980s and 1990s.

Threatened with prison on trumped-up nonsense

charges aiming to break up the movement, Don Phau steadfastly refused to plead guilty, despite notorious offers to many defendants that if they left politics they would be spared. Under pressure, his wife left him and took away his two sons.

It was likely during the five years that this quietly humorous and loving man was in a Virginia penitentiary, or shortly after his release from this barbarism, that the disease that would kill him, Multiple Sclerosis, came to afflict him.

But Don went back into action. Under great harassment and with meager resources, Don helped organize Lyndon LaRouche's 2000 Presidential campaign. The overriding theme was to counter the national nightmare: Al Gore, leading the Democrats' surrender to New Age insanity, and George W. Bush, preparing to install a dictatorship under cover of some provocation like Hitler's Reichstag fire.

Over many years Don persisted in political and historical work with dazzling optimism, refusing to yield, though increasingly frail from the crushing effects of his auto-immune disease.

In February and March, just days before he died, he was still working through his research findings on the amazing humanistic program that General Douglas MacArthur brought to Japan during America's post-World War II military occupation.

Don Phau is survived by Deborah Sonnenblick, his partner for the past ten years and, in the later days, his devoted caregiver; his two sons Peter and Paul Phau; his niece C. Alexis Freeman; and hundreds of admiring friends, co-workers, and readers.

Donald Phau: When America Started Downhill

This appeared in Executive Intelligence Review, *May 8, 2015.*

In April 1968, Robert F. Kennedy was on a plane heading for a campaign rally in Indianapolis when he was told that Martin Luther King was shot dead. He was told to call off the rally. The chief of police warned him not to go into the ghetto. His police escort abandoned him as he entered the ghetto. The crowd that gathered had not heard the news of King's death. Kennedy told them. He ended: "Let us dedicate ourselves to what the Greeks wrote so many years ago: To tame the savageness of man and make gentle the life of the world. Let us dedicate ourselves to that."

Over the next days there were riots in 110 cities. Thirty-nine people were killed, mostly black. There were 75,000 troops in the street. There were no riots in Indianapolis where Kennedy was campaigning. He went to Cleveland and said, "Violence goes on and on. Why? What has violence accomplished? What has it ever created? No martyr's cause has ever been stilled by his assassin's bullet."

RFK's biographer writes: "He flew back to Washington, a city of smoke and flame, under curfew, patrolled by troops. He walked through the Black districts. Burning wood and broken glass were all over the place. Walter Fauntroy said, 'The troops were on duty. A crowd followed behind us, following Bobby Kennedy. The troops saw us coming at a distance, and they put on gas masks and got their guns at ready, waiting for this horde of Blacks coming up the street. When they saw it was Bobby Kennedy, they took off their gas masks and let us through. They looked awfully relieved.'"

During the worst of the urban riots of 1967 Kennedy, though advised not to, toured the Black and Hispanic areas. When asked what he would do if he became President, Kennedy said he would make the media show what it was like to live in the ghettos. He said: "Let them show the soul, the feel, the hopelessness, and what it's like to think, you'll never get out. Show a Black teenager, told by some radio jingle to stay in school, looking at his older brother who stayed in school and is out of a job. Show the Mafia pushing narcotics; put a candid camera team in a ghetto school and watch what a rotten system of education it really is.... Ask people to watch it—and experience what it was like to live in the most affluent society in history—without hope."

On June 6, 1968, RFK won the California primary and was heading for the Presidency. That day he was shot dead.

—Donald Phau